The How-to-Cook Book

Marguerite Patten

HAMLYN

London · New York · Sydney · Toronto

Contents

Acknowledgements
These black and white photographs are by courtesy of:
British Egg Information Service,
Frying an egg page 13
Making pancakes, page 62
Flour Advisory Service,
Curate's eye, page 13
Hot lamb pies, page 42
Golden apricot pudding, page 69
Australian Recipe Service,
Rump steak Melbourne, page 47
Lard Information Bureau,
Barbecued turkey pie, page 41
Coffee Promotion Service,
Coffee for breakfast, page 16
Dutch Dairy Bureau,
Janhagel, page 77
Eden Vale Ltd.,
Cottage cheese and pineapple salad, page 59
Heinz,
Festival Alaska, page 69
White Fish Authority,
Halibut with Gorgonzola, page 35
Scallops of fish Florentine, page 35
Stork Cookery Service,
Asparagus and cheese sauce, page 55

First published in the LEISURE-PLAN series in 1970 by
The Hamlyn Publishing Group Limited
London · New York · Sydney · Toronto
Astronaut House, Feltham, Middlesex, England
© Copyright The Hamlyn Publishing Group Limited 1974

ISBN 0 600 34410 X
Printed in England by Chapel River Press, Andover,
Hampshire

The cover shows thick vegetable broth (see page 24),
pork chops garnished with apple slices and tomato
baskets (see page 38) and lemon meringue pie (see page 67).

Photography by John Lee
Line drawings by Jackie Grippaudo

Useful facts and figures

Oven Temperatures

The following chart gives the conversions from degrees Fahrenheit to degrees Celsius (formerly known as Centigrade) recommended by the manufacturers of electric cookers.

Description	Fahrenheit	Celsius	Gas Mark
Very cool	225	110	$\frac{1}{4}$
	250	130	$\frac{1}{2}$
Cool	275	140	1
	300	150	2
Very moderate	325	170	3
Moderate	350	180	4
Moderately hot	375	190	5
	400	200	6
Hot	425	220	7
	450	230	8
Very hot	475	240	9

Note This table is an approximate guide only. Different makes of cooker vary and if you are in any doubt about the setting, it is as well to refer to the manufacturer's temperature chart.

Comparisons of Weights and Measures

It is useful to note that 3 teaspoons equal 1 tablespoon; the average English teacup is $\frac{1}{4}$ pint; the average English breakfast cup is $\frac{1}{2}$ pint; and a B.S.I. measuring cup, used in recipes, holds $\frac{1}{2}$ pint or 10 fluid ounces.

It should be noted that the American pint is 16 fluid ounces, as opposed to the British Imperial and Canadian pints which are 20 fluid ounces. The American $\frac{1}{2}$ pint measuring cup is 8 fluid ounces, and is therefore equivalent to $\frac{2}{5}$ British pint. In Australia the British Imperial pint, 20 fluid ounces, is used for liquid measures. Solid ingredients, however, are generally calculated in the American cup measure. In America, standard cup and spoon measurements are used.

American Terms

The list below gives some American equivalents or substitutes for terms used in this book.

biscuits	cookies
castor sugar	granulated sugar
courgettes	zucchini
frying pan	skillet
gherkins	sweet dill pickles
greaseproof paper	wax paper
grilled	broiled
minced	ground
spring onions	scallions
Swiss roll pan	jelly roll pan

Metrication

For quick and easy reference when buying food, it should be remembered that 1 kilogramme (1000 grammes) equals 2·2 pounds ($35\frac{3}{4}$ ounces) – i.e. as a rough guide, $\frac{1}{2}$ kilogramme is about 1 pound. In liquid measurements 1 litre (10 decilitres or 1000 millilitres) equals almost exactly $1\frac{3}{4}$ pints (1·76), so $\frac{1}{2}$ litre is $\frac{7}{8}$ pint. As a rough guide, therefore, one can assume that the equivalent of 1 pint is a generous $\frac{1}{2}$ litre. Where an accurate conversion is necessary only decilitres are given. Where less important the rounded litre figure is also included.

A simple method of converting recipe quantities is to use round figures instead of an exact conversion, taking 25 grammes to 1 ounce, and a generous $\frac{1}{2}$ litre to 1 pint. Since 1 ounce is exactly 28·35 grammes and 1 pint is 568 millilitres, it can be seen that these equivalents will give a slightly smaller finished dish, but the proportion of liquids to solids will remain the same and a satisfactory result will be produced.

1 dl. (decilitre) = 100 ml. (millilitres).

Secrets of successful cooking

Enjoy food
One of the most important secrets of successful cooking is to *enjoy* your food. This means it is essential to shop well for good quality fresh food and prepare it well. Develop a good palate by tasting your own and other people's cooking, criticise these mentally so that you know *why* it is good or *why* it is *not* good.

Have confidence in yourself
If you *are* new to cooking (and this book is planned especially for those of you who are starting to cook for the first time) do *not* doubt your ability to create interesting and appetising dishes. With a little bit of know-how, practice and the will to succeed you will become a good cook in a very short time.

Follow recipes carefully
Cooking is a matter of common sense and the willingness to follow recipes until you are able to form your own ideas. May I suggest, therefore, that you work through recipes without altering them to begin with, except of course for minor adjustments in seasoning, then you will be able to adapt them for your own particular tastes.

Make food look appetising
Take time and trouble to make the cooked food look interesting and colourful. Suggestions for garnish or decoration are given in the various recipes.

Use the right technique for handling or cooking
One of the important things to appreciate in preparing dishes is that the *right* technique in both *mixing* ingredients and *cooking* the food makes a great deal of difference. Certain words are used to describe the putting together of the ingredients i.e. folding or blending and if you are uncertain as to *exactly* what they mean, I suggest you turn to the end of the book where they are clearly defined. It is also important to appreciate the reason why simmering is used when cooking some foods (slower cooking than boiling); definitions of cooking processes are on page 7.

Buy good utensils
Kitchen utensils are of great importance in preparing food and in the chapter on equipment and utensils you will see how one should buy utensils and having bought them, how you should look after them. It is important to use your utensils correctly and to use the correct utensil for each job; for example, when a recipe suggests you chop parsley finely you will find it quite easy if you use a proper chopping knife, or gadget for this purpose but extremely difficult if you try to chop it with an ordinary table knife. When you are told to fold ingredients together, a metal spoon or palette knife will do this successfully whereas a wooden spoon will be too heavy for this rather delicate handling.

How does one plan a good menu? The answer is fairly simple – choosing:
Foods that are plentiful and in season.
Foods you and your family like.
Foods you can afford.
Foods that are good for you.

Having formulated the idea of what kind of dishes you would like, put them together as an interesting nutritious and practical menu.

A good menu should provide a variety of flavours, for example, if you start a meal with a cream of chicken soup, you do not serve chicken as a main course, but you should have meat or fish to follow. If you plan chicken with a cream sauce as a main course you need a non-creamy soup or an hors d'oeuvre which has more colour and a slightly more definite flavour. Do not have a first course that is so strong in flavour that it completely ruins one's palate for the dishes that follow.

Another important aspect of menu planning is to make certain that you have not chosen dishes that all need last minute preparation. This is particularly important when you are new to cooking. For example, in a three-course meal it would be sensible to have a cold hors d'oeuvre, or a soup that could be prepared beforehand and reheated. Your main course could be a hot one which means you will have to dish up meat or fish, vegetables and gravy or sauce. The dessert could be cold and of the type that is prepared well beforehand and only needs bringing to the table.

Foods that are necessary to good health
Food should be enjoyed, but should also be good for one, therefore, during a day it is important to ensure that menus contain a selection of important foods:
Protein In fish, meat, eggs, cheese, peas, beans and lentils; to ensure healthy growth in children and main-

tain strength in adults. Every main meal should have some kind of protein food.

Fats In butter and other fats; to create a feeling of warmth, particularly necessary in cold weather.

Carbohydrates Sugar – in sugar itself and anything containing sugar; in honey, golden syrup, and of course natural sugars are found in fruit. Starches – in flour and foods made with flour, some vegetables, e.g. potatoes, peas, beans.

Carbohydrates taken in reasonable quantities give energy, if taken in excess quantities they cause over-weight.

Minerals Two of the most important are iron – in liver, heart, kidney, flour, eggs, cocoa, black treacle, dried fruits (such as apricots and prunes) and in dark green vegetables such as spinach to create healthy red blood, and calcium – in cheese and milk to help build healthy bones and strong teeth.

Vitamins

A In butter, margarine, eggs, liver, carrots and green vegetables, also herrings and other oily fish; to pro-mote healthy growth.

B In wheat germ and yeast and yeast extract; to pre-vent a feeling of tiredness.

C In many fruits (particularly citrus, blackcurrants and rosehips), lightly cooked or raw green vegetables; to give a healthy skin.

D Found in most of the same foods as Vitamin A (except green vegetables) and also in sunlight. It helps to form strong teeth and bones and enables the body to absorb calcium.

Shopping for food

Food is an expensive commodity and it is, therefore, important to shop wisely so that money is not wasted. When choosing a shop these are the points to watch: Look at local shops and make certain that they are kept clean.

That they have a quick sale for perishable items, for this ensures the food will be fresh.

That the assistants are careful in their handling of food. When you shop for food, check on the following:

Cheese

Cheese that is stale has a hard outside and this indi-cates that it has been exposed to the air for too long a period. See the section on cheese (page 71).

Fish

Fish should have a pleasant smell, the scales and eyes should look bright. If there is a smell of ammonia it is an indication that the fish is stale. In small fishmonger's shops it is often wiser to choose fish that is freshly caught and in season, rather than having very definite and pre-conceived ideas as to what you should and should not buy. For example, you may want to follow a recipe which mentions plaice. If plaice is not avail-able or not very good, it is quite likely that the same recipe could be followed with small portions of fresh haddock or fillets of whiting or, for a special occasion, fillets of sole.

Fruit

Fruit should look fresh and be unbruised. Soft fruits, such as strawberries and raspberries, should look dry; if the bottom of a punnet is damp it indicates that the fruit could be very soft on the lower layer.

Meat

Raw meat should look freshly cut and moist. A dry, hard outside indicates that the meat has been exposed to the air for too long a period. Be prepared to ask the butcher questions about various cuts but choose a day when he is not too busy. Information on this is given on page 36. Cooked meat deteriorates quickly when exposed to the air for a long period, so watch that cooked ham, tongue or other meats, are not dry and hard. Most modern stores, shops and supermarkets have cold cabinets for cooked meats which keep them as fresh as possible.

WISE BUYING

As indicated above, it is wise to buy in reliable shops and to get fresh food; it is also important to study prices. Many stores have special offers on certain food (often canned or packaged foods that do not deteri-orate) so make use of these.

Sometimes it is worthwhile buying larger quantities of food, particularly if it is not perishable. For example, a small size can of a certain food may cost 8p but a can containing double the ingredients may only be 14p, so giving a saving of 2p. It is, however, very im-portant to make certain that the whole of the large can will be used, for if there is a possibility of any of the food being wasted it is, obviously, no longer a bargain.

STOCKING YOUR LARDER

For the purpose of this book, I have assumed you have a refrigerator and I have divided the food between highly perishable items which go into a refrigerator and those foods which you can store without any particular conditions. If, however, you have no re-frigerator, obviously, all foods will have to be kept in your larder which means that you will shop more frequently and take particular care over storage.

A well stocked larder is a means of providing food which will help you plan menus without last minute shopping. Here are some of the foods that you would be wise to store:

Canned foods Have a selection of soup, fish, meat, fruit and vegetables.

Beverages Tea, coffee, cocoa, chocolate. It is important that coffee in particular is bought freshly and whether you use ground or instant is a matter of personal taste.

Biscuits Both sweet and savoury, bought or home-

made. Make certain the tin for storing is airtight.

Bouillon cubes or stock cubes To use when you have no stock available.

Bread Which should be kept in a bread container or tin, or loosely wrapped in foil. It should never be kept with biscuits, cakes or pastry. Allow good air circulation around bread.

Breadcrumbs The crisp variety are known as raspings and are sold in packets. It is obviously cheaper to make your own by crisping left-over pieces of bread very slowly in the oven and then rolling them into fine crumbs and storing in jars.

Condiments Often referred to in recipes as seasonings. Salt, pepper, mustard and vinegar are the most usual but other flavourings could be kept, such as Worcestershire sauce, Tabasco sauce and tomato ketchup.

Cornflour and custard powder These are the more usual things but some recipes require arrowroot and a small amount of this can also be kept.

Flour Either all plain, or self-raising or both plain and self-raising.

Peas or beans (dried) These are, however, often superseded by canned or frozen.

Rice, spaghetti and other pasta

Sugar Various kinds of sugar are mentioned in recipes:
Castor Necessary for light textured cakes.
Demerara or moist brown Both are brown sugars.
Granulated Slightly cheaper than castor and can be used for cooking fruit.
Icing sugar Needed for cake icings.
Loaf sugar For table use.
Preserving sugar (a form of loaf sugar) For jam making. In addition, golden syrup, black treacle, honey and jam are generally stored in the larder. Make certain that you do not leave half-filled tins or jars of jam for any length of time since the air can cause these to spoil.

STOCKING YOUR REFRIGERATOR

Care must be taken to appreciate the difference between an ordinary domestic refrigerator and a deep freeze, which is in most food stores and shops, and a home freezer. The latter stores food for a very much longer period than an ordinary refrigerator. It is, however, worthwhile mentioning that the frozen food compartment (where ice is made) of a refrigerator varies in the time it allows frozen food to be stored. A star system has been evolved whereby one star means that frozen food may be kept for one week in the frozen food compartment; two stars mean it may be kept one month; three stars mean it may be kept up to three months. Frozen food should never be kept in the ordinary cabinet of the refrigerator unless you wish it to defrost slowly.

The general rule is to cover all foods, except raw meat, so that they do not dry. Foods with strong smells, such as fish, should be kept at the top of the cabinet – this minimises intermingling of smells. Never put hot food or hot liquid into the cabinet. Milk and all dairy produce should be stored, well covered, in the proper racks or fairly high in the cabinet. Butter and fats should be covered and kept in the special compartment. Cooked meats and uncooked bacon must be well wrapped to prevent drying. Hard cheese, such as Cheddar, may be stored in a refrigerator if well covered. Soft cheese, such as Camembert, should never be refrigerated – keep it in the larder.

Raw meat is highly perishable and should not be kept for more than 1–2 days in a refrigerator. The same applies to fish.

Salads and green vegetables should go into the proper salad containers or into polythene bags. Keep tomatoes covered in the same way but try not to put them with lettuce.

Frozen foods, including ice cream, should go into the frozen food compartment.

Ice is made by filling the freezing trays with water.

CONVENIENCE FOODS

This is the title given to modern foods which are prepared ready to be heated, cooked or served at once.

Dried foods Many modern dried foods, or to give them their correct title Accelerated Freeze Dried (AFD), are foods which are frozen and then dried. This prevents the long soaking which used to be necessary with dried foods in the past. Soups, sauces and complete meals are obtainable in this form.

Canned foods Practically every form of food both simple and exotic is now obtainable in cans. When once a can has been opened the food is highly perishable. Foods may be stored in opened cans for a short time except for fruit; the syrup of this turns cloudy when stored in the can so transfer to another container.

Frozen food Be critical when buying frozen food. Every frozen food cabinet has a demarcation line and this is the height to which frozen food should be stored. Some shopkeepers are less fussy than they could be so do not buy frozen food when it is piled above the line because defrosting, i.e. melting, could have taken place. Frozen foods are obtainable in a wide variety – vegetables, meat, fish, cakes and desserts. Follow the instructions for use as given on the pack and for storage according to the manufacturer's instructions and your own particular conditions. When frozen food has thawed out or has been cooked it is highly perishable and should be treated as such.

Handling food

Before food can be cooked or served it needs, in most cases, some special preparation.

Bacon It is a good idea to cut off the rinds on bacon rashers before cooking; if frying the bacon put these into the pan with the rashers to provide extra bacon fat. If boiling salted bacon, soaking will be necessary.

Cheese One is often told to grate cheese and this means rubbing the cheese (choose as hard a piece as possible) against a grater or putting it into a special grating utensil.

Eggs In many recipes one is told to break the egg. The easiest way to do this is to crack the shell sharply on the edge of a plate or saucer and gently pull the shell apart so that the whole egg drops into a cup or saucer. Never hold the egg too high above the utensil otherwise you tend to break the yolk.

In some recipes one is told to separate the yolk from the white. This is quite a difficult thing to do when you first begin cooking. You crack the shell as above but do not pull the halves of the egg shell apart. Instead, you let the white trickle into the basin and then gently pull the egg shells apart so that the yolk remains in one half of the shell. Tip the empty shell over the utensil so any extra white can run out. Pour the yolk into this emptied shell and if any white remains in the second half add this to the utensil.

Fish Wash in cold water before cooking, dry well on kitchen paper. Some recipes talk about filleting fish. The way to do this is as follows:
1 Choose a really sharp knife (special filleting knives are obtainable).
2 Put fish on a chopping board and cut off the head.
3 Make a sharp cut down the centre; feel the backbone with the knife.
4 Hold the fish firmly with the left hand; a little salt on your fingers gives a good grip. Insert the knife tip under the flesh; ease this away from the backbone for the first fillet.
5 Repeat on the other side.
6 Turn fish over and repeat stages 3–5.
Sometimes one is told to skin fillets; to do this:
1 First dip the knife and your fingers in a little salt. Hold the tail end of each fillet firmly: make a cut near the end.
2 Insert the tip of the knife under the cut; ease flesh away slowly and carefully from the skin.

Meat As meat is handled a great deal, it is always advisable to wash it in cold water before cooking and dry well on kitchen paper. In hot weather, 2–3 drops vinegar in the water freshens meat. It must be stressed, however, that if meat is not particularly fresh nothing will make it safe to eat.

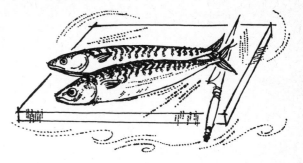

Poultry Two terms have been given when referring to poultry; the first one is to draw the bird which means removing the stomach and liver, this will be done for you by the butcher; the second term is to truss and if the butcher has not done this it simply means tying or skewering the legs of the bird to the body to give a neat shape in cooking. Wash poultry or game as meat and dry inside and out very thoroughly.

Vegetables Most vegetables need special preparation and as this varies so much, details are given on pages 55–58.

CONSISTENCIES

The word consistency is used to describe the softness of mixtures, generally it is applied to a cake or scone mixture but the first three terms in this list are applied to sauces:

Thin sauce This is barely thickened and generally means using 1 oz. (25 g.; $\frac{1}{4}$ cup) flour to 1 pint (575 ml.; $2\frac{1}{2}$ cups) liquid.

Coating consistency So that the sauce just coats the back of a wooden spoon. Generally this means using 1 oz. (25 g.; $\frac{1}{4}$ cup) flour to $\frac{1}{2}$ pint (275 ml.; $1\frac{1}{4}$ cups) liquid.

Thick or panada consistency Very thick, generally used to bind ingredients together. This means 1 oz. (25 g.; $\frac{1}{4}$ cup) flour to $\frac{1}{4}$ pint (150 ml.; $\frac{2}{3}$ cup) liquid.

Pouring consistency Softest of all. The mixture pours easily from the bowl into the tin.

Soft dropping consistency Drops from the spoon within about 3 seconds.

Firm or slow dropping consistency Drops from the spoon when given a sharp flick.

Sticky consistency Too soft to roll but firm enough to stand in points when handled with a palette knife.

Soft rolling consistency So that the mixture is rather elastic but can be rolled with a floured rolling pin.

Firm rolling consistency So that the mixture can be rolled out easily without using a great deal of flour on the pastry board.

COOKING METHODS

There are certain terms used in cooking to denote the method by which heat is applied to food, a number of descriptions are given below:

Baking Cooking in dry heat in the oven. Success is

achieved by using the right heat and right position in the oven.

Boiling Cooking by immersing the food in a pan of liquid, which must be kept boiling gently all the time.

Braising Almost a combination of stewing and roasting. Meat is browned in fat then placed on a bed of vegetables called a mirepoix with a little liquid surrounding, in a covered vessel and cooked slowly in the oven or on top of the cooker, gradually to break down the meat tissues.

To casserole Not a basic method, but means cooking slowly in the oven in a covered casserole dish.

Shallow frying Cooking in hot fat in an open pan.

Deep frying Cooking by immersing food in a deep pan of hot fat.

Grilling Cooking quickly under a hot grill; used for tender pieces of meat and fish.

Poaching Cooking gently in water which is just below boiling point; used for eggs or fish.

Pressure cooking Cooking in a special tightly closed container under pressure at a higher temperature than usual; food is cooked much more quickly than normal.

Roasting Cooking with a little fat in a hot oven. Fat is poured from the baking pan over the meat or poultry from time to time, using a long-handled spoon: this is known as basting – often people say true roasting can only be done on a spit.

Simmering The rate of cooking used for stews, just below boiling point, so that the liquid bubbles gently at the side of the pan.

Steaming Cooking either in a steamer over a pan of boiling water, or in a basin standing in (but not covered by) boiling water.

Stewing Cooking slowly until the food is tender. It is done in just enough liquid to cover the food, as the liquid is served with it and should be rich. Stews may be cooked in covered saucepans or casseroles, but always at a low temperature.

Kitchen equipment

The kitchen may be said to be the workshop of any home and as such it is a very important place. It is worthwhile, therefore, spending money on good equipment and good utensils. The most important equipment that you buy for your kitchen would be:

THE COOKER

Take a great deal of time in selecting the kind of cooker you feel would be adequate for your requirements. Many people buy too small a cooker and have problems when they have guests. On the other hand it is very unwise to have a cooker that is too large if your family is a very small one throughout most of the year. Learn how to use the cooker with the help of the manufacturer's instructions. You may find occasionally this varies from the instructions in this and other

books. This is because all cookers vary within a certain amount. The chart of oven temperatures on page 3 will give you guidance as to the average temperature.

Here, however, are some general points to remember.

The hot plates or burners Hot plates on electric cookers today are easy to control and so are gas burners. You will find in the previous chapter a description of the various methods of cooking and it is important to learn the correct position on which you can achieve rapid boiling without fear of the food spilling over, or gentle simmering.

The grill Modern grills are hot and quick. Even so in many cases it is advisable to pre-heat the grill for a few minutes before food is put under. This means that you get quick cooking and/or browning and the food is not over-cooked or dried.

The warming cabinet It is difficult to discuss the warming compartment of cookers since they vary considerably. Some have a heating drawer. In others (generally electricity) you heat the plates in a compartment above the oven. Make full use of any capacity you have for heating plates, for hot food quickly becomes cold if it is served in cold dishes or on cold plates.

The following chart shows the positions in a gas or electric oven and the kind of foods which would be put into these temperature zones:

Gas	Electricity
Top	**Top**
Hottest Use for small cakes, scones, Yorkshire puddings.	*Hottest* Use for small cakes, scones, Yorkshire puddings.
Centre	**Centre**
Less hot Use for meat pies, large cakes.	*Coolest* Use for casseroles, large cakes, custard.
Bottom	**Bottom**
Coolest Use for casseroles, milk puddings, custard.	*Slightly less hot* in most cookers than top. Use for meat pies. Cook on floor or just above floor of oven, depending on your cooker.

THE REFRIGERATOR

Packing your refrigerator is discussed on page 6. It is, however, very important to defrost the refrigerator as instructed by the manufacturer. In most cases it is when the ice round the freezing compartment becomes nearly $\frac{1}{2}$ inch (1 cm.) thick. It is also important to keep the cabinet scrupulously clean. Do not use detergent in the water since that could give a smell to the cabinet which could be transmitted to the food. I like to add 1 tablespoon of bicarbonate of soda or a few drops of vinegar to every 2 pints (generous litre, 5 cups) of water used in washing out the refrigerator.

Never store foods in a refrigerator unless this is operating properly otherwise you do not have the correct air circulation.

KITCHEN UTENSILS

I have not listed the kitchen equipment in the order of importance for this varies. A good selection of knives could be very important in one home and less important in another.

Tools for cutting

Knives Always select knives critically to see they are easily held and the right size for you. These are the important knives you will need (there will be many others that can be added):
1 Vegetable knife.
2 A larger knife for chopping, generally called a cook's knife.
3 A broad-bladed knife (palette knife) for lifting food out of pans, turning food, as well as binding ingredients together.

As well as these three knives one generally needs a knife in the kitchen rather like a dining room knife for spreading fat, buttering bread. A knife with a pointed end is very inefficient for this purpose.
4 A bread knife, preferably with a serrated edge.
5 Carving knife.
6 Vegetable parer. Remember if you are left-handed you can get one designed for you.

Other tools for cutting are:
1 Various chopping utensils – look at these in ironmongers' stores. They are useful for chopping parsley, onions and other vegetables.
2 Can opener. There are various kinds available from the rather simple type to the more elaborate wall type.
3 Kitchen scissors which remove the rinds from bacon much more easily than a knife.

OTHER KITCHEN UTENSILS

Mixers, dishwashers, waste disposal units An electric mixer, whether the large type or small portable type, is a very useful addition to kitchen equipment. The whisks and beaters help in whisking, and creaming. Follow the directions given by the manufacturer as to whether the bowl should be warmed when creaming fat.

The blender or liquidiser is for emulsifying ingredients to give:
1 A smooth purée of vegetables or fruit and very largely takes the place of a sieve except it does not remove pips from tomatoes, raspberries and similar foods.
2 For chopping parsley, making breadcrumbs for stuffing and coating foods.
3 For emulsifying ingredients for mayonnaise (see page 53).

Some mixers have more complex attachments such as shredders and slicers.

A dishwasher and waste disposal unit These are useful aids in a kitchen, as are coffee percolators, electric frying pans and electric kettles.

COOKING UTENSILS

Saucepans These can be selected in cast iron, aluminium, stainless steel and in modern ceramic ware. You need:
1 A saucepan for milk and sauces with a pouring lip if possible.
2 Several larger saucepans for vegetables.
3 A large pan for boiling pieces of bacon. In addition you also need strainers and a colander; a double saucepan for cooking foods such as egg custards, is always extremely useful.
4 Casseroles that can be put in the oven are convenient. It is, however, possible to have ceramic ware, etc., which can be used both as a saucepan and a casserole.
5 Pie dishes and other ovenproof ware for various pies and puddings.
6 Frying pan. One just large enough to take big fillets of plaice and other foods and it is advisable to have either a second frying pan or a special pan for omelettes and pancakes.
7 Steamer. A two- or three-tier steamer which enables you to cook a complete meal.
8 Cake tins of various shapes, including a tin that could be used for a Yorkshire pudding.

EQUIPMENT FOR HANDLING FOOD

Basins and mixing bowls For blending and mixing ingredients.
Cutters For cutting pastry or scones into various

shapes. One generally uses a plain cutter for savoury purposes and a fluted cutter for sweet dishes.

Dredger Ideally one should have two, one for flour and one for sugar. Useful for giving an even coating on the pastry board or on the food itself.

Fish slice For lifting fish and other foods out of the pan.

Grater Choose one with several sizes.

Moulds For jellies.

Pastry board and/or chopping board Remember modern laminated surfaces can mark if you chop food on them so a chopping board is always advisable.

Pastry brush For brushing egg on food to glaze it, also for brushing fat on to tins.

Rolling pin For rolling out pastry.

Scales To make certain weights are quite accurate.

Sieve For putting food through to give a smooth purée, or for removing lumps from flour, icing sugar, etc.

Spoons You need wooden spoons for mixing certain foods, but metal kitchen spoons are always useful.

Squeezer For extracting juice from lemons and oranges.

Storage jars Airtight ones for storing coffee, etc.

Strainer For straining sauces and gravies.

Tongs For lifting and handling food.

Various kitchen papers Foil or transparent cooking paper for protecting food in the oven or in the refrigerator. Kitchen paper or kitchen roll for draining fried food, wiping the excess fat out of frying pans, and similar tasks. Greaseproof (wax) paper for lining cake tins.

Vegetable brush For cleaning vegetables.

Whisk For whisking egg whites.

LOOKING AFTER EQUIPMENT AND UTENSILS

The golden rule is to clean soiled equipment such as the cooker as quickly as possible before grease has a chance to set. The oven is always easiest to clean if wiped out when warm.

Saucepans, roasting tins, frying pans Put these to soak immediately after use. If a saucepan has been used for milk or eggs, cold water should be used to prevent the protein coagulating and becoming more difficult to remove. Clean with special pads, never use soda in aluminium or stainless steel pans. A roasting pan or frying pan which is used with fat should be wiped out with paper before washing (a roasting pan has not been included in the list of equipment because it is supplied with the cooker, but covered roasters are also obtainable see page 39). An omelette pan should not be washed on the inside. It should be wiped out with soft paper immediately after use, this prevents any possibility of omelettes sticking. Clean non-stick pans as recommended by the manufacturers.

Knives If used, stainless steel knives require little cleaning. With other knives clean with an abrasive cleaner and dry very well.

Wooden spoons, rolling pins Always wash these in warm detergent solution and dry well.

What went wrong?

Soups and sauces

If the soup or sauce was lumpy, the flour was inadequately blended; whisk hard or strain through a sieve.

If the soup or sauce is too thick, either too little liquid was added or the soup or sauce cooked for too long a period in an open pan. Stir in a little extra liquid.

If the soup or sauce tasted too salty, probably the salt was added without tasting. Whisk in a little milk or cream, or simmer a sliced raw potato in the soup or sauce for 10 minutes. It then absorbs the salt.

Fish dishes

If the fish breaks in handling, it was over-cooked or inadequately coated before cooking. Shape neatly again before serving.

If the fish was dry and tasteless, it was probably over-cooked. Serve with a good sauce or with melted butter.

Meat dishes

If the meat was tough, it was either inadequately cooked or it was the wrong cut for quick cooking. Either cook for a longer period or mince or chop and put into an interesting sauce.

If the meat was dry and hard, it was either over-cooked or cooked too slowly, or insufficient fat was used. Serve with a gravy sauce to restore the moist texture.

Salads and vegetables

If a salad was limp in texture, the salad greens were not shaken dry or the oil and vinegar was put on too long before serving. There is little one can do.

If vegetables lacked flavour, they were over-cooked or cooked in too much water. All one can do is to season them well and add a good amount of butter.

Pastry

If the pastry is tough, too much water was used and the pastry was over-handled.

If the pastry breaks badly, either too little liquid or too much fat was used. In either case there is little one can do except correct the fault next time.

Cheese dishes

If a cheese mixture, such as cheese sauce or Welsh rarebit is very tough or stringy the cheese is over-cooked. There is little one can do.

Biscuits

If biscuits are soft, either they were under-baked or the tin in which they were stored was not airtight. Reheat for a short time in a moderate oven, cool, then put into a tightly sealed tin.

Techniques used in handling foods

Beating Another word for the movement used in creaming and whisking. It means you mix the ingredients together with a very brisk movement, either to make them smooth, or to incorporate air. Use the utensils as suggested under creaming and whisking.

Blending Used for mixing the ingredients in some sauces, for custard, or when adding flour to liquid. It means you mix the ingredients together thoroughly until the mixture is smooth and free from lumps. A wooden spoon is used.

Chopping Used to prepare vegetables and meat for cooking; parsley or other herbs for garnish. It means to cut food into small pieces. Use a sharp knife and a chopping board. When chopping parsley, steady the knife by placing a finger on the top of the knife near the point, then move the handle clockwise.

Creaming Used to blend fat and sugar for cakes; to give a smooth purée of vegetables. It means to soften a mixture until the consistency of cream e.g. when potatoes are mashed they are often described as *creamed* potatoes. To cream fat and sugar means to beat them until they are soft and light, so incorporating air. Use a wooden spoon and stand the basin on a folded tea cloth to prevent it moving on the table. Work in a clockwise direction but when your arm begins to ache, stop, and give one or two turns in an anti-clockwise direction, which rests your arm.

Flaking Used in preparing cooked fish for various dishes, such as fish cakes. It means to divide the fish into small pieces. In this way you have a more attractive appearance than if fish was chopped.

Folding Used to add flour to eggs and sugar in a sponge; sugar to egg whites in a meringue. It means to flick an ingredient into others already beaten and so avoid losing air. Use a metal spoon or palette knife and a very gentle movement from the wrist. Beating flour into a sponge rather than folding means you will lose the light, fluffy texture. If you feel that you are too vigorous when folding the ingredients together, hold your wrist firmly but lightly with the forefinger and thumb of your other hand. This restricts vigorous movement and then you have the correct amount of movement for gentle folding.

Kneading Used in handling bread, biscuit or pastry dough. It means working the ingredients together lightly with your hands. It is essential to knead the dough well in bread making by pulling and stretching, using the base of the palm (often called the heel). In this way the yeast is distributed evenly throughout the bread dough. The way to test if dough is kneaded sufficiently, is to press gently and firmly with the tip of the finger. Insufficiently kneaded dough means the impression of the finger will be left; with well kneaded dough, the impression comes out slowly but completely.

Kneading of biscuit dough may be done quite firmly. Kneading of pastry dough is simply a gentle gathering together of the ingredients before rolling.

Rolling out Used for making pastry, biscuit or yeast dough the required shape and thickness. Pastry in particular can be spoiled by heavy, rather than light rolling, so hold the rolling pin firmly but lift it once or twice as you roll. Lift the dough from the table or pastry board frequently to prevent it becoming sticky in rolling. Do not roll pastry dough in all directions otherwise it is stretched and you have a badly shaped pie or flan. Roll ahead, then lift and turn the pastry dough at right-angles and roll again, until you get the desired shape.

Rubbing in Used in preparing short crust pastry; some biscuits; some cakes (e.g. rock cakes); the crumble mixture for topping fruit. It means to mix fat and flour with your fingers until the mixture is like breadcrumbs. Use either the tips of your fingers or just the forefinger and thumb of each hand. Lift the mixture in the air when you rub in so as the crumbs drop back again into the bowl they incorporate a certain amount of air. This keeps the ingredients cool and helps to lighten them. Never rub fat into flour with the palms of the hands, otherwise the mixture becomes sticky and hard.

Whipping Used for cream. It means to beat until the mixture is thickened, a similar action to whisking and the word is sometimes used instead of whisking. Cream is whipped to thicken it. Care must be taken that it is not over-whipped. A fork or egg whisk is used.

Whisking Used for egg whites to make them stiff. It means to handle ingredients briskly in a circular movement to incorporate air and in doing this they become stiff. An egg whisk is generally used.

11

Breakfast time

Although many people find they do not need a cooked breakfast, it is important to have something sustaining at the beginning of the day, especially if you have a long journey and facilities are limited for a good mid-day meal.

Growing children in particular should have protein if possible, in the form of eggs, bacon or fish. Often the reason why a cooked or protein food is not eaten at breakfast time is lack of time, so lay the table the night before if possible and put everything ready.

Fruit
Fresh grapefruit is ideal for breakfast time, halve the grapefruit, remove the pips and separate the segments. To do this, loosen the segments from the skin and the centre.

Grapefruit and orange cocktail (allow 1 grapefruit and 3 oranges for 4 servings): Cut away the peel and pith from the fruit. Insert the knife between the skin and the segments of fruit and cut these away, discarding any pips. Put the segments of orange and grapefruit into four glasses.

Fruit juice
Squeeze fresh orange juice into glasses or serve canned grapefruit, orange, pineapple or tomato juice.

Cooked fruit
Serve cooked prunes, apples or other fruit, see page 70.

Cereals
Serve packet cereals with sugar and hot or cold milk.

PORRIDGE

Cooking time is dependent upon the type of rolled oats.

IMPERIAL · METRIC	AMERICAN
3 oz./75 g. medium or coarse oatmeal	$\frac{1}{2}$ cup medium or coarse oatmeal
$\frac{1}{2}$ teaspoon salt	$\frac{1}{2}$ teaspoon salt
$1\frac{1}{2}$ pints/$\frac{3}{4}$ litre water	$3\frac{3}{4}$ cups water

Serves 4

Put the oatmeal and salt into a basin. Gradually stir in the cold water until evenly mixed. This can then stand for several hours if wished. Put into a saucepan or preferably the top of a double saucepan, bring to the boil or bring the water in the base of the double saucepan to the boil. Cook for at least 1 hour in a saucepan, $1\frac{1}{4}$ hours in the top of a double saucepan. Stir during cooking. Serve with salt or sugar and hot or cold milk.

CURATE'S EYE

Cooking time: 5 minutes

IMPERIAL · METRIC	AMERICAN
4 slices bread	4 slices bread
3 oz./75 g. butter	6 tablespoons butter
4 eggs	4 eggs
4 tomatoes	4 tomatoes

Serves 4

Cut a circle out of each slice of bread approximately $2\frac{1}{2}$ inches (6 cm.) in diameter. Heat 1–$1\frac{1}{2}$ oz. (25–40 g.; 2–3 tablespoons) butter in a pan. Fry the bread circles until crisp and brown; drain and put on hot plates. Butter both sides of the slices of bread and put into the frying pan. Fry until crisp on the one side, turn, then break the four eggs carefully and lower into the middle of each slice; cook as for fried eggs.

Meanwhile, slice and cook the tomatoes – if there is not room in the pan these can either be served raw or cooked in a separate pan, or sliced and put into the oven for a short time. Serve the tomato slices on the rounds of fried bread.
Note Butter is used in this recipe to fry the bread, but fat can be used on other occasions.

BOILED EGGS

IMPERIAL · METRIC
1 or 2 eggs
water

AMERICAN
1 or 2 eggs
water

Cooking time: see table

Serves 1

Use a rather small saucepan; water in which eggs are boiled discolours aluminium saucepans so you may like to keep one pan for this purpose. Put in enough cold water to cover the egg (or eggs). This generally means that the saucepan is half filled. There are two ways of boiling eggs as shown in the table. If you wish to start from cold, put egg gently into the cold water, time from the point water starts to boil, otherwise bring water to boil then lower egg into water. Time carefully, then when cooked remove egg from water, put into egg cup.

To prevent dark line forming around hard-boiled egg yolks When a hard-boiled egg is served cold it some-times has an unsightly dark line around the yolk, this is caused by over-cooking. To prevent this, lift the egg from water when cooked, crack shell lightly (to allow steam to escape) and plunge it into cold water.

Cooking times

	Really soft-boiled egg	Firm-set egg	Hard-boiled egg
If put in cold water	3 minutes	4 minutes	10 minutes
If put in boiling water	4 minutes	5 minutes	10 minutes

FRIED EGGS

IMPERIAL · METRIC
1 or 2 eggs
butter or other fat (see method)

AMERICAN
1 or 2 eggs
butter or shortening (see method)

Cooking time: few minutes

Serves 1

Break the eggs carefully on to saucers. Heat the fat in the pan; butter gives an excellent flavour if cooking the eggs fairly slowly, but you may prefer to use fat left from frying bacon or cooking fat. Use approximately ½ oz. (15 g.; 1 tablespoon) fat for 1 egg, but 1 oz. (25 g.; 2 tablespoons) fat is enough for 2–3 eggs (it should just give a thin covering over the base of the pan). If you want a crisp white of egg then have the fat very hot; for a soft egg white just heat the fat so the egg sets within 30 seconds of being put into the pan. If the fat is too cool then the egg white spreads over the base of the pan and makes it almost impossible to remove the eggs. Cook steadily for several minutes until white and yolk are set. To cover the yolk, spoon over a little fat, this gives a thin white covering to the yolk which many people like. Lift out of the pan with a fish slice and serve with grilled or fried bacon and tomato.

Curate's eye

Frying an egg

POACHED EGGS

Cooking time: few minutes

Serves 2

IMPERIAL · METRIC
2 slices bread
$\frac{1}{2}-\frac{3}{4}$ oz./15–20 g. butter or margarine plus
    a little extra if using poacher
2 eggs
seasoning

AMERICAN
2 slices bread
1–1½ tablespoons butter or margarine
    plus a little extra if using poacher
2 eggs
seasoning

Put serving plates to warm first. Toast the bread and spread with butter or margarine, then keep hot while cooking the eggs. To cook in an egg poacher: put water in the bottom of an egg poacher. Grease two of the small metal cups with butter or margarine. Heat until the water is boiling. Break an egg into an ordinary cup. If you wet the cup first you will find the egg pours out more easily. Pour into a metal cup, repeat with second egg and cover the poacher with a lid. Cook for 2–3 minutes until the egg white sets. Slide from the metal cups on to toast. Serve at once.

To cook in a pan of water: half fill a saucepan or frying pan with water. Add a pinch of salt, and bring the water to the boil. Then turn down the heat so that the water boils steadily. Break the eggs into a wet cup, and slide them into the boiling water.

If you stand a greased plain round pastry cutter in the water, you can pour the egg into this and the white keeps a good shape, or 2–3 drops of vinegar added to the water helps to prevent the white from spreading. Cook for 2–3 minutes, until the white sets. If using a cutter, lift this out first, then remove the egg with a fish slice. Hold the slice and egg over the water for a few seconds to drain, so that you do not make the toast wet. Put the egg on to the buttered toast, repeat with second egg and serve at once.

SCRAMBLED EGGS

Cooking time: few minutes

Serves 2

IMPERIAL · METRIC
2 slices bread
$\frac{1}{2}-\frac{3}{4}$ oz./15–20 g. butter or margarine for
    toast
2–3 eggs
seasoning
1 tablespoon milk (optional) or single
    cream
$\frac{1}{2}-1$ oz./15–25 g. butter or margarine for
    eggs
Garnish
parsley

AMERICAN
2 slices bread
1–1½ tablespoons butter or margarine for
    toast
2–3 eggs
seasoning
1 tablespoon milk (optional) or coffee
    cream
1–2 tablespoons butter or margarine for
    eggs
Garnish
parsley

Put serving plates to warm first. Toast the bread and spread with butter or margarine. Keep warm on the plate while cooking the eggs. Break the eggs into a basin, season, add the cream or milk if wished; (this gives a softer but less rich mixture). Whisk with a fork. Melt the butter or margarine in a saucepan. Add the egg and milk. Turn the heat very low and cook slowly. Stir with a wooden spoon, moving the egg from the bottom of the pan all the time, until the mixture begins to thicken. Remove the pan from the heat, for the egg continues to cook in the hot saucepan. Never allow scrambled eggs to become too set. Pile on to hot toast and put a sprig of parsley on top. Serve at once. When serving scrambled eggs as a supper dish you may like to increase amount of eggs to two per person.
Note It is easier to wash the saucepan if you put it to soak at once in cold water.

BACON AND SAUSAGES

Cooking time: 10–15 minutes

Serves 1

IMPERIAL · METRIC
1–2 sausages
1–2 bacon rashers
fat, if frying

AMERICAN
1–2 sausages
1–2 bacon slices
shortening, if frying

Prick the sausage skins lightly, although some modern sausage skins do not burst if they are left un-pricked, this is a wise precaution.
To grill Put the sausages on the grid of the grill pan or in the pan itself. Large sausages take approximately 15 minutes, smaller sausages take 10 minutes. Remove the rinds from the bacon and add to the sausages about 4 minutes before serving. Turn the sausages several times with two knives or tongs so they become evenly brown.

To fry Add only ½ oz. (15 g.; 1 tablespoon) fat to the frying pan, heat, then put in the pricked sausages and cook for approximately the same time as grilling, then add the bacon.

To fry tomatoes Halve the tomatoes – allow 1–2 per person. Season lightly and cook in the hot fat remaining in the pan after cooking the bacon. It is advisable to cook the tomatoes after the egg if possible, as the liquid from the tomatoes may cause the eggs to stick to the pan.

To grill tomatoes Put the halved, seasoned tomatoes in the grill pan. Brush with a little fat or top with a very small piece of margarine or fat. Heat for a few minutes under the grill before putting the bacon and sausages on the grid.

To fry mushrooms Wash the mushrooms well. If very perfect do not skin as the skin contains a great deal of flavour. Remove the stalks if wished, or leave them on and just cut the base. Cook steadily for 5–6 minutes in the hot fat, turning over once or twice.

To grill mushrooms Follow the directions for tomatoes but be fairly generous with the fat in the grill pan as mushrooms dry easily.

FISH CAKES

Cooking time: 8–10 minutes

Serves 4–6

IMPERIAL · METRIC	AMERICAN
8 oz./200 g. cooked white fish (poached or steamed)	½ lb. cooked white fish (poached or steamed)
8 oz./200 g. mashed potato	1 cup mashed potato
seasoning	seasoning
1 egg, beaten	1 egg, beaten
Coating	**Coating**
1 oz./25 g. flour	¼ cup all-purpose flour
seasoning	seasoning
1 egg, beaten	1 egg, beaten
4 tablespoons crisp breadcrumbs (raspings)	⅓ cup dry bread crumbs
4 oz./100 g. fat for frying	½ cup shortening for frying
Garnish	**Garnish**
parsley	parsley
lemon	lemon

Remove all the bones and skin from the fish, flake with a fork. Add the potato, seasoning and egg. Mix well, then divide into four to six portions. Form each of these into a flat cake on a pastry board and neaten with a palette knife. Coat the fish cakes in seasoned flour, then in egg and crumbs. Heat the fat in a frying pan, fry the fish cakes until golden brown on the underside. Turn and cook on the second side. Lift out of the pan, drain on absorbent paper. Serve hot, garnished with parsley and lemon.

SMOKED HADDOCK

Cooking time: 10 minutes

Serves 2

IMPERIAL · METRIC	AMERICAN
1 small smoked (Finnan) haddock or 8–12 oz./200–300 g. smoked haddock fillet	1 small smoked (Finnan) haddock or about ½ lb. smoked haddock fillet
½ pint/250 ml. water, or half milk and half water	1¼ cups water, or half milk and half water
1 oz./25 g. butter or margarine	2 tablespoons butter or margarine

Cut the fins and tail from the whole haddock and divide into two portions (or cut the fillet into two portions). Put the water, or milk and water, into a shallow saucepan or frying pan. Add the fish, bring up to the boil and lower the heat. Simmer for 3–5 minutes if thin, or up to 6–7 minutes for thicker pieces of fish. (Do not over-cook smoked haddock. It is cooked when the fish breaks away from the bone if it is tested with a knife.) Lift out with a fish slice – hold over the pan for 1 minute so the fish drains. Put on to a hot dish, top with butter or margarine and serve.

Many people like to top smoked haddock with a poached egg.

To cook kippers

Kippers may be cooked in several ways, one of the most successful is jugged kippers (this causes less smell than other ways).

Put the kippers (with fins and tail removed if wished) into a tall jug or dish and cover with boiling water. Put a cloth over the container to keep in the heat. Leave for 5 minutes, lift out the kippers and drain, then serve topped with a knob of butter or margarine.

Fried kippers Put ½ oz. (15 g.; 1 tablespoon) of fat in a frying pan and fry the kippers steadily for 5–6 minutes or until tender.

Grilled kippers Heat the grill, brush each kipper with ½ oz. (15 g.; 1 tablespoon) melted fat and cook under a hot grill for 5–6 minutes.

SAUTE POTATOES

Cooking time: 6–8 minutes

Serves 1–2

IMPERIAL · METRIC
1 oz./25 g. fat
2 medium-sized boiled potatoes
Garnish
1 teaspoon chopped parsley

AMERICAN
2 tablespoons shortening
2 medium-sized boiled potatoes
Garnish
1 teaspoon chopped parsley

Heat the fat in a pan. Cut the potatoes into neat slices and fry for 3–4 minutes: turn over and fry for the same time on the second side. Lift on to absorbent paper (kitchen roll is excellent) to drain. Serve hot topped with chopped parsley.

BREAKFAST PIZZA

Cooking time: 30–35 minutes
Oven temperature: 425°F.,
220°C., Gas Mark 6–7

Serves 4

IMPERIAL · METRIC
Scone dough
12 oz./300 g. self-raising flour

2 teaspoons salt
3 oz./75 g. butter or margarine
about ¼ pint plus 3 tablespoons/200 ml. milk
Topping
1 14-oz./400-g. can tomatoes, well drained
8 chipolata sausages
4 eggs

AMERICAN
Scone dough
2 cups all-purpose flour sifted with 2¼ teaspoons baking powder
2 teaspoons salt
6 tablespoons butter or margarine
about ½ cup milk
Topping
1 14-oz. can tomatoes, well drained
8 sausages
4 eggs

Sift together the flour and salt. Rub in two-thirds of the butter or margarine until mixture resembles fine breadcrumbs. Gradually add the milk and bind together to form a soft dough. Roll out to a round 10 inches (26 cm.) in diameter and place on a baking sheet. Make four deep wells for the eggs using the back of a tablespoon. Melt the remaining butter or margarine and use some to brush over the top. Spread tomatoes on the top of the scone dough between the wells and leave a ½-inch (1-cm.) border round the outside. Arrange sausages radially from centre, two between each well.

Bake in a hot oven for 30–35 minutes; 10 minutes before the end of the cooking time carefully drop an egg into each well from a cup. Pour a teaspoon of the remaining melted butter or margarine over eggs and return to oven until the eggs are just set.

Coffee for breakfast

TO MAKE COFFEE

Infusion time: few minutes –
this varies with the method

You will need
ground coffee · water · milk

Buy only a small quantity of coffee at a time, and if possible have it freshly ground. The ideal way is to buy the coffee beans, and to grind the coffee yourself as you need it. But for this you must have a coffee grinder. When you are choosing coffee, buy the best you can afford. Mocha coffee, which comes from Aden and Mocha, is generally considered to be the best, but you will find by experience which brands you prefer. If you like your coffee with a strong flavour choose one to which a little chicory has been added. When you store your coffee, take care that it is not near any strong-smelling foodstuffs, as it quickly absorbs other odours and is spoilt. When you open a can or a packet (if you have bought the vacuum-packed kind, and not had it freshly ground) immediately transfer the coffee to a screw-topped jar. This keeps it fresh. Use sufficient coffee: about 4 tablespoons to 1 pint (generous $\frac{1}{2}$ litre; $2\frac{1}{2}$ cups) water. Use freshly drawn water, as for tea making. Never allow the coffee to boil with the water, bring it just to boiling point. Add hot, not boiling milk or single cream to coffee.

Breakfast coffee is usually a lighter roast than after-dinner coffee and is sometimes known as American roast. For after-dinner or black coffee, choose the darker kind; this is sometimes called Continental roast and is much stronger and richer in flavour.

One generally allows $\frac{1}{2}$ pint (250 ml.; $1\frac{1}{4}$ cups) coffee and $\frac{1}{2}$ pint milk for two people for breakfast (this gives them two cups each of fairly milky coffee). For tiny after-dinner cups allow $\frac{1}{4}$ pint (125 ml.; $\frac{2}{3}$ cup) coffee for two people, plus a little milk or cream.

To make coffee in a jug
Warm the jug. Put in the coffee (quantity as given above). Pour over the freshly boiling water. Give a brisk stir, cover and leave for a few minutes. Strain into a second hot jug or into cups.

To make coffee in a percolator
Choose medium ground coffee for a percolator. Fine ground coffee forms too solid a block and it is difficult for the water to penetrate. Quantity as above. Put in the water. Put the coffee into the basket. Either stand the percolator on the cooker or plug it in if using an electric model. Allow to come to the boil, reduce the heat so the liquid percolates gently through the basket. With a thermostatically controlled percolator you can set it and the coffee percolates itself and never boils too fast.

To make coffee in a saucepan
Put the water into the pan, bring to the boil, add the coffee (or heat the coffee and water together taking care it does not boil for any length of time), stir and remove from the heat. Keep in a warm place to infuse for 3–4 minutes, strain into a hot jug.

To make coffee by the filter method
Place the coffee in the upper container and pour the boiling water over the coffee. The hot coffee then gradually filters through into the bottom container.

To make instant coffee
In these days many people make instant coffee and the directions are given on the container. It should, like all coffee, be freshly made so that you have the flavour at its best.

TO MAKE TEA

Infusion time: few minutes

You will need
tea · water · milk

The most important thing to remember is to take the teapot to the kettle, and not the kettle to the teapot. Pour water from the cold tap into the kettle and put it on to heat. Take the teapot over to the kettle and when the water is hot, but not boiling, pour a little into the teapot to warm. Just before the water is boiling pour the water out of the teapot and put in the tea.

For one person put in 2 teaspoons tea (the old adage 1 teaspoon per person and one for the pot is still a wise one) so for four people you would put in 5 level tea-spoons of tea for a really strong brew. If you like weak tea you can use a little less. Immediately the water in the kettle boils, turn or switch off the heat. With an electric kettle, pull out the plug after switching off the electricity. Hold the kettle firmly; then pour the boiling water steadily over the tea. Put the lid on the teapot and let it stand for several minutes. Some people like to stir the tea, then let it stand. The leaves fall to the bottom of the pot and the tea is ready to be poured, through a tea-strainer if possible.

Cream of cauliflower soup (see page 24)

Lunch or dinner

In many homes, this is the most important meal of the day and it needs careful preparation and thought.

Read the suggestions about menu planning (see page 4) so that the main meal does not prove too difficult.

First courses

Generally called an hors d'oeuvre although some people like to call it an appetiser. You can serve:

Fruit juices See suggestions for breakfast, but make the fruit juice look more interesting by balancing a slice of lemon or orange on the edge of the glasses. To do this make a small slit in each slice of orange or lemon and press this on the rim of the glass. Put a small sprig of mint into a glass of tomato juice if you like.

Fruit See suggestions for breakfast, in addition:

Melon Cut slices of ripe melon, remove seeds, then decorate each slice with a cherry on a small plastic or wooden cocktail stick. Serve with spoon and fork or fruit knife and fork.

Avocado pear Halve, remove stone and fill centre with French dressing or with a few shelled prawns, blended with mayonnaise. Allow half an avocado pear and 1 oz. (25 g.; 1 tablespoon) shelled prawns per person. If prepared beforehand sprinkle the cut pear with lemon juice to prevent it becoming brown.

EGG HORS D'OEUVRE

Omelettes Serve small portions of an omelette or a small omelette. This is particularly suitable before a cold main course.

Baked eggs See the recipe below.

Hard-boiled egg mayonnaise See salads (page 54).

BAKED EGGS

Cooking time: 10–15 minutes
Oven temperature:
375–400°F., 190–200°C.,
Gas Mark 5–6

Serves 1

IMPERIAL · METRIC	AMERICAN
½ oz./15 g. butter	1 tablespoon butter
2 tablespoons single cream	3 tablespoons coffee cream
1 egg	1 egg
flavouring (optional, see below)	flavoring (optional, see below)

Rub a small ovenproof dish with half the butter and add half the cream. Break the egg carefully into the dish, add a very little seasoning, then cover with the rest of the cream and the last of the butter. Bake for 10 minutes, if you like a very lightly set egg, or 15 minutes for a firmer egg, towards the top of a moderately hot oven. Serve in the baking dish with a teaspoon.

Flavourings Add 2–3 chopped canned asparagus tips to the cream before adding the egg. Sprinkle the top of the egg with 1 oz. (25 g.; ¼ cup) grated cheese before adding the cream and butter.

FISH AND SHELLFISH HORS D'OEUVRE

Serve small portions of any of the fish dishes in the book (allow approximately half the usual amount).

Fish salads Serve small portions of the salads given in the book (see pages 59–61).

Rollmop herrings Serve 1 rollmop herring (obtainable in jars) with a wedge of lemon and garnish with 1–2 lettuce leaves.

Smoked salmon Allow 1½–2 oz. (40–50 g.) smoked

salmon per person. Arrange on plates with wedges of lemon, garnish with lettuce leaves and serve with brown bread and butter and cayenne pepper.
Smoked eel As smoked salmon, allow 2 oz. (50 g.) per person. Serve with bottled horseradish cream.

Smoked trout Allow 1 smoked trout per person. Serve on the plate with a wedge of lemon, garnish with lettuce. Serve with horseradish cream and brown bread and butter. The heads are generally removed, but it is usual to lift away the skin before serving.

PRAWN COCKTAIL

Serves 4

IMPERIAL · METRIC	AMERICAN
4–6 oz./100–150 g. peeled prawns or about 1½ pints/¾ litre prawns in their shells	⅔–1 cup peeled prawns or shrimp or about 3¾ cups in their shells
4–6 lettuce leaves (use the heart if possible)	4–6 lettuce leaves (use the heart if possible)
6–8 tablespoons mayonnaise	½–1 cup mayonnaise
2 teaspoons tomato purée (you buy this in a tube or can) or 1 tablespoon tomato ketchup	2 teaspoons tomato paste or 1 tablespoon tomato catsup
2–3 drops Tabasco sauce (optional)	2–3 drops Tabasco sauce (optional)
1 tablespoon cream or top of the milk	1 tablespoon cream
seasoning	seasoning
Garnish	**Garnish**
2 teaspoons chopped parsley	2 teaspoons chopped parsley
1 lemon	1 lemon

If using peeled prawns they may be frozen, so allow to defrost at room temperature. If in a hurry put the packet into cold water until thawed. To peel prawns (or shrimps), drop them into hot water for about 1 minute, then lift out and remove heads and shells (they come away very easily when the fish is warm). Shred the lettuce finely, remember this will be eaten with a teaspoon. Put the lettuce into glasses or dishes.

Blend the mayonnaise with the rest of the ingredients, except the garnish; toss the prawns in this and put on the lettuce. Top with chopped parsley. Cut off slices of lemon, make a small slit in each slice and balance on the edge of the glasses.

MEAT HORS D'OEUVRE

Salami Serve small portions of sliced salami, garnished with lettuce and a small piece of tomato. Allow 2 oz. (50 g.) per person.
Ham Serve 1–2 oz. (25–50 g.) ordinary cooked ham, or the rather expensive smoked Parma ham with a slice of fresh melon, a halved peeled ripe pear or a canned or fresh fig. Serve with cayenne or paprika pepper.
Pâté Serve portions of pâté, either bought, canned or

home-made with slices of hot toast and butter. Allow approximately 2 oz. (50 g.) per person. Garnish with a wedge of lemon and lettuce leaf.
Note In many recipes a wedge of lemon is mentioned, this makes it easier to squeeze out a generous amount of juice, than with a thinner slice. Slices, however, are often a more attractive garnish.

PATE

Cooking time: 45 minutes
Oven temperature:
325–350°F., 170–180°C.,
Gas Mark 3–4

IMPERIAL · METRIC	AMERICAN
12 oz./300 g. calf's liver	¾ lb. calf's liver
seasoning	seasoning
1–2 bacon rashers	1–2 bacon slices
1 egg	1 egg
4 tablespoons double cream	⅓ cup whipping cream
1 oz./25 g. butter for dish and paper	2 tablespoons butter for dish and paper

Serves 5–6

Put the liver through a mincer, if you have no mincer then scrape the liver with a sharp knife until smooth in texture, this is not difficult to do. Rub the blade of the knife against the liver on a board and you will gradually bring away pieces of meat, almost as finely as if the liver had been minced.

Put into a basin, add the seasoning, then the minced

or finely chopped bacon, egg and cream. Put into 1-pint (½-litre) buttered dish and cover with buttered paper. Stand the dish in another larger dish or pan of cold water (this prevents sides hardening) and bake for 45 minutes. Cool without removing the buttered paper.

If using a rather deep dish allow about 10 minutes longer cooking time.

MIXED HORS D'OEUVRE

A very pleasant mixed hors d'oeuvre can be made with flaked, canned or fresh salmon, prawns, sliced salami, diced ham, sliced cooked sausages, portions of various salad, sliced hard-boiled eggs, bottled olives, gherkins, cocktail onions, coleslaw and sweetcorn.

Making soups

A good soup is an excellent start to a meal, and is not difficult to prepare. Certain terms are used in preparing soups and this is what they mean:

Stock This is a liquid obtained from boiling bones. For white stock cover the well-washed bones of chicken (carcass) or veal with cold water. Add a good pinch of salt and shake of pepper. Cook for approximately 1 hour or longer, strain carefully, store in cool place. Brown stock is made in the same way but use beef bones (a good marrow bone is ideal). Vegetables may be added if wished but if they are, a stock keeps less well.

Note Stock is a highly perishable commodity. Stock cubes (often called meat or bouillon cubes) may be added to water to give an instant stock, or use vegetable or beef extract to flavour the water.

Bouquet garni This is a small bunch of mixed herbs – sage, parsley, thyme, rosemary, chives, tied together with cotton and put into the soup to give flavour. A pinch mixed dried herbs could be substituted.

Some types of soup you will find recipes for in this book:

Consommé A clear unthickened soup (see page 23).
Cream soups A creamy white sauce is blended with the purée (see page 24).
Purée soups Where the mixture is put through a sieve or put into an electric blender until a smooth pulp or purée (see page 23).

Garnishes for soup

Blanched almonds Suitable for most soups. Put almonds into boiling water for $\frac{1}{2}$–1 minute, then skin. Excellent on chicken soup.
Chopped parsley Wash and dry small sprigs parsley. Put on to a board and chop with a sharp knife. The best way to chop parsley is to steady the tip of a sharp knife with a finger of your left hand, then to rotate the knife backwards and forwards, chopping as you do so. If preferred, use a pair of kitchen scissors or put the parsley into the blender.

CROUTONS

Cooking time: 3 minutes

Serves 4–6

IMPERIAL · METRIC
2 slices bread ($\frac{1}{4}$ inch/$\frac{1}{2}$ cm. thick)
1 oz./25 g. butter or fat

AMERICAN
2 slices bread ($\frac{1}{4}$ inch thick)
2 tablespoons butter or shortening

Remove the crusts from the bread and cut into $\frac{1}{4}$-inch ($\frac{1}{2}$-cm.) cubes. Heat the butter or fat in a frying pan. Toss the pieces of bread in this until golden brown.

Drain on absorbent paper. Put into a small dish or sprinkle on to the soup just before serving. Suitable for most soups.

CHEESE AND ONION SOUP

Cooking time: 15–20 minutes

Serves 4

IMPERIAL · METRIC
1 pint (generous $\frac{1}{2}$ litre) water with 1 or 2 chicken stock cubes or 1 pint/generous $\frac{1}{2}$ litre chicken stock
1 oz./25 g. butter
1 large onion
1 oz./25 g. flour
2 oz./50 g. Gouda cheese, diced
Garnish
parsley

AMERICAN
2$\frac{1}{2}$ cups water with 1 or 2 chicken bouillon cubes or 2$\frac{1}{2}$ cups chicken stock
2 tablespoons butter
1 large onion
$\frac{1}{4}$ cup all-purpose flour
scant $\frac{1}{2}$ cup diced Gouda cheese
Garnish
parsley

Dissolve the stock cube in hot water in a saucepan, or heat the stock. Melt the butter in a pan and fry the peeled and finely chopped onion until brown. Add the flour and cook for a few minutes without colouring.

Gradually blend in stock. Simmer for 5–10 minutes and add diced cheese just before serving. Garnish with chopped parsley.

Glazed bacon (see page 38)

CONSOMME

A real consommé is made by cooking beef with water, then straining the liquid carefully, but a simple consommé may be made from this recipe.

Cooking time: 15 minutes

Serves 4

IMPERIAL · METRIC
1 small onion
2 beef or chicken stock cubes
1½ pints/¾ litre water
bouquet garni
1–2 tablespoons dry sherry

AMERICAN
1 small onion
2 beef or chicken bouillon cubes
3¾ cups water
bouquet garni
1–3 tablespoons dry sherry

Peel the onion and put all the ingredients, except sherry, into the saucepan. Heat gently until the stock cubes are dissolved, then simmer for 10 minutes. Strain or lift out the onion and herbs. Add sherry and serve.

Garnishes for consommé Cooked vermicelli, cooked diced vegetables or tiny pieces of cooked chicken (in a chicken consommé).

DRIED PEA SOUP

Cooking time: 1½ hours

Serves 4–5

IMPERIAL · METRIC
8 oz./200 g. dried peas
2 pints/generous litre bacon stock*
2 onions
1 carrot
1 turnip
seasoning
1 teaspoon sugar
sprig mint or pinch dried mint
Garnish
2 bacon rashers

AMERICAN
generous 1 cup dried peas
5 cups bacon stock*
2 onions
1 carrot
1 turnip
seasoning
1 teaspoon sugar
sprig mint or pinch dried mint
Garnish
2 bacon slices

*When you have stock left from boiling a piece of bacon, try to use it in a soup like this, because the flavour is excellent. A lentil soup, or vegetable soup can be made with bacon stock too with very good results.

Soak the peas overnight in the bacon stock. Put into saucepan with the peeled and diced vegetables, seasoning, sugar and mint and simmer gently for approximately 1¼–1½ hours. Either rub through a sieve or beat until very smooth. Taste and re-season. Garnish with crisp pieces of grilled or fried bacon.

Lentil soup
Use 6–8 oz. (150–200 g.; scant 1 cup) lentils in place of dried peas; 8 oz. (200 g.; 1 cup) lentils makes a really thick soup.

GAIETY SOUP

Cooking time: few minutes

Serves 4

IMPERIAL · METRIC
1 15½-oz./385-g. can cream of tomato soup
1½–2 oz./40–50 g. demi-sel or cream cheese
about 2 teaspoons milk
pinch garlic salt
small savoury biscuits or crackers
salted almonds

AMERICAN
1 15½-oz. can cream of tomato soup
about ¼ cup demi-sel or cream cheese
about 2 teaspoons milk
pinch garlic salt
small savory crackers
salted almonds

Heat the soup according to the directions on the can. Blend the cheese with the milk and garlic salt until soft and creamy. Pipe or pile the cheese on to small biscuits or crackers and garnish with salted almonds or other large nuts. Pour the soup into a hot serving dish and float the biscuits on the top *immediately* before serving to prevent these becoming soft.

CREAM OF TOMATO SOUP

Cooking time: 1¼ hours

Serves 4–5

IMPERIAL · METRIC
1 lb./½ kg. tomatoes
1 onion
1 carrot
1 stick celery
2 oz./50 g. streaky bacon rashers
1½ pints/¾ litre stock or water
seasoning
bouquet garni
½ oz./15 g. cornflour or 1 oz./25 g. flour

½ pint/250 ml. milk
pinch sugar
Garnish
grated Parmesan cheese
croûtons (page 21)

AMERICAN
1 lb. tomatoes
1 onion
1 carrot
1 stick celery
3 bacon slices
3¾ cups stock or water
seasoning
bouquet garni
2 tablespoons cornstarch or ¼ cup
    all-purpose flour
1¼ cups milk
pinch sugar
Garnish
grated Parmesan cheese
croûtons (page 21)

Skin the tomatoes (see page 56). Peel the onion and carrot, slice the vegetables and chop the bacon. Fry the bacon slowly to extract the fat, then add the vegetables and fry for about 10 minutes over a low heat. Add the stock or water, seasoning and bouquet garni, bring to the boil and simmer gently until tender – about 1 hour. Remove the bouquet garni, rub the soup through a fine sieve, and add the cornflour or flour blended with the milk. Return to the pan, *bring just to the boil*, stirring well, and cook gently for 2–3 minutes, *do not boil*. Season, add sugar and garnish.

Alternative method
Cook the vegetables with the bacon, stock, herbs and seasoning and sieve. Meanwhile, make a white sauce with 1 oz. (25 g.; 2 tablespoons) butter, 1 oz. (25 g.; ¼ cup) flour and ½ pint (250 ml.; 1¼ cups) of milk in another saucepan. Cook until thickened. Reheat the tomato mixture and whisk the hot tomato mixture into the hot sauce. With this method there is no risk of the soup curdling.

OTHER CREAM SOUPS

Follow the recipe for cream of tomato soup with the following modifications:
Cream of asparagus soup Use a medium can of asparagus instead of tomatoes. Other ingredients are the same except omit the bacon and carrot.

Cream of cauliflower soup Use a small cauliflower cut into small pieces, instead of tomatoes. Omit carrot. Garnish with parsley and paprika. (Illustrated on page 18)
Cream of vegetable soup Use 1 peeled potato, 2 tomatoes, 4 oz. (100 g.; 1 cup) fresh peas, instead of all tomatoes. Other ingredients are the same.

THICK VEGETABLE BROTH

Illustrated on the jacket

Cooking time: 25–30 minutes

Serves 4

IMPERIAL · METRIC
1¼ lb./¾ kg. mixed vegetables*
1 oz./25 g. pearl barley or rice
seasoning
1½ pints/¾ litre stock or water with
    2 chicken stock cubes
Garnish
chopped parsley

*carrots, potatoes, swede, beans, peas,
    tomatoes, leeks

AMERICAN
1¼ lb. mixed vegetables*
scant ¼ cup pearl barley or rice
seasoning
3¾ cups stock or water with 2 chicken
    stock cubes
Garnish
chopped parsley

*carrots, potatoes, swede, beans, peas,
    tomatoes, leeks

Peel and cut the vegetables into small dice or grate them very coarsely; beans should be cut in neat pieces, tomatoes should be skinned. If using pearl barley, blanch by putting it into cold water, bring water to boil and cook for 1 minute. Strain, cook in boiling salted water until tender, approximately 20 minutes. If using rice cook in boiling salted water until soft, approximately 15 minutes. Meanwhile, put the vegetables and stock in a pan and cook until tender, this will vary according to how large the pieces are but will take from 10–20 minutes. Add the barley or rice to the vegetable mixture, reheat, then serve garnished with chopped parsley.

READY PREPARED SOUPS

Canned These just need reheating. Add herbs to give interest or top with a little cream.

Dehydrated Always blend the soup powder carefully with the water and cook for the recommended time.

Cooking fish

The way you can tell if fish is fresh is given on page 5 together with suggestions for good shopping. On the following pages you will find various fish listed and how it should be cooked for the best results.

The basic methods of cooking begin on page 29.

White fish (Salt water fish)

Kind of fish and how to buy		Best ways of cooking
Bass	Whole or cut into steaks or fillets.	Poach, steam, fry, grill or bake.
Bream	(Can also be fresh water bream) whole or filleted.	Grill or bake.
Brill	Rarely used whole as it is a large flat fish. Normally filleted.	As plaice.
Cod	Small codling whole, larger fish filleted and bought in portions or cut across to give cutlets, often called steaks.	An ideal fish to cook in every way.
Flounder	Small flounder generally bought whole.	As plaice.
Haddock	As cod.	As cod.
Hake	As cod.	As cod.
Halibut	A more expensive white fish. Small halibut rarely caught – bought whole. Larger fish cut into slices called cutlets. A filling fish so buy less than usual.	Best methods are poaching, grilling or frying.
Dogfish or Huss	A very economical fish, sold skinned and filleted. A large-boned fish, so be generous in the amounts bought.	Bake or fry.
John Dory or Dory	Generally sold filleted.	As plaice.
Plaice	Although obtainable throughout the year, during December to May the fish is full of roe which detracts from its flavour.	Can be cooked by any method – steaming, poaching, frying or grilling.
Skate	An ugly fish sold in irregular shaped portions, normally triangular. Large round pieces (eye-balls of fish) also sold.	This delicious fish can be poached, baked or fried. As it is solid and slightly tough in texture steam for 5 minutes before frying.

Kind of fish and how to buy		Best ways of cooking
Sole	As plaice, although more expensive.	As plaice.
Turbot	Distinguished from halibut by spots on skin. Buy as halibut.	As halibut.
Whiting	Very light textured fish easy to digest, so ideal for small children and invalids. Buy whole or filleted.	As plaice.

Oily fish

Kind of fish and how to buy		Best ways of cooking
Herrings	Although obtainable from various sources throughout the year, British herrings are rather full of roe and therefore less good from March to May. Generally bought whole, easier to eat if boned and filleted.	Grill, fry, bake, pickle or souse.
Mackerel	Larger than herrings. All fish is dangerous if eaten stale, but mackerel can cause severe stomach upsets. Buy as herrings.	As herrings.
Mullet	Grey or red mullet. A small fish bought whole.	Best baked or grilled. Use plenty of fat as its texture is dry. Liver of mullet can be cooked with the fish.
Salmon	An expensive fish, the finest being Scotch. When sold out of season it is imported frozen. Large fish sold in slices called cutlets or steaks.	Normally poached and used hot or cold. Can be grilled or baked and occasionally fried.
Salmon trout	Smaller than salmon, bought and cooked whole.	As salmon.
Sprats	A small fish similar to herrings.	Grill, fry or bake.
Whitebait	Very tiny fish, similar to herrings.	Do not remove heads before cooking. Always fry.

Beef cobbler (see page 45)

Smoked fish

Kind of fish and how to buy		Best ways of cooking
Smoked cod	Large cod are filleted then smoked. Buy in portions.	As haddock.
Smoked haddock	Often described as Finnan haddock. Small haddock split and smoked whole. Larger fish filleted, then smoked.	Poach in water or cook in milk in oven. Can be topped with poached egg.
Kippers	Split, salted and smoked herrings.	May be grilled, fried, poached in water, or baked in oven.
Bloaters	Smoked whole herrings, not split.	As kippers.
Buckling	A form of smoked herring.	Serve as smoked trout.
Smoked salmon	Cut in wafer thin slices. Very expensive.	Never cook. Serve raw at the beginning of a meal with brown bread and butter and lemon, or in sandwiches.
Smoked sprats	Whole.	Grill or fry.
Smoked trout	Whole.	Always serve raw as smoked salmon at the beginning of a meal with lemon, brown bread and butter, and horseradish sauce if you wish.
Smoked whiting	Filleted and smoked often called golden fillets.	As smoked haddock.
Smoked eel	A very unusual smoked fish becoming better known. Buy either portions or whole, smoked eel, or filleted smoked eel.	Serve raw as smoked salmon.

Shellfish (Crustaceans)

Kind of fish and how to buy		Best ways of cooking
Clams	Generally sold out of shells or canned.	Generally put into a soup or sauce.
Cockles	Generally bought ready cooked and out of shells.	Served cold with bread and butter.
Crab	Generally bought ready cooked.	If not prepared (dressed being the correct term) remove flesh from shell and claws. Discard the thin stomach bag and grey brown fingers which must not be eaten. Serve cold in salads, occasionally cooked as lobster.
Crawfish (Langouste)	Like lobster but no claws.	As lobster.
Crayfish	A small freshwater fish like lobster.	As lobster.
Lobster	Generally sold cooked. A good lobster feels heavy for its size. If it feels light it is full of water and not a good buy.	Generally served cold in salads, although it can be put into hot sauce.
Mussels	Sold in shells by the fishmonger or in jars ready prepared.	Scrub shells. Discard any which do not close tightly when tapped. Put into pan with cold water, little seasoning, parsley; heat gently until shells open. Remove fish from shells, cut away hairy growth, serve as first course.
Oysters	In shells, the fishmonger will open them for you. Sold by the dozen. Expensive.	Eaten raw, swallowed whole. Served with brown bread and butter, lemon, paprika or cayenne pepper. Sometimes added to sauces.
Prawns	Generally sold cooked, sometimes ready shelled.	Often served cold in salads, or added to sauces.
Scallops	Occasionally called escallops. Sold on shells by fishmonger.	Remove from shells, wash very thoroughly. Poach in a little milk until tender, then add milk to white sauce.
Scampi	The name given to large prawns.	Generally coated in egg and crumbs or batter and fried.
Shrimps	As prawns.	As prawns.
Whelks	Generally sold cooked.	Remove from shells with a pin.
Winkles	Like small whelks.	As whelks.

Freshwater fish

Kind of fish and how to buy		Best ways of cooking
Carp	Generally whole.	Best baked slowly, as rather tough for other methods of cooking. Generally stewed.
Eel	Very popular. Fish-mongers keep them in tanks so they can be killed, cut, skinned and sold fresh. Can be bought in jelly.	
Trout	Whole.	Grill, fry or bake. As a dry fish use plenty of fat.
Perch	Generally whole. Cut away very sharp fins before cooking.	Plunge into boiling water for 1 minute then remove scales. Best fried or grilled.
Bream	See under white fish.	

Fish roes

Kind of fish and how to buy		Best ways of cooking
Cod's roe	Fresh, uncooked.	Steam for approximately 10 minutes. Skin. Add to sauces or slice and fry in fat.
	Fresh, ready cooked.	Add to sauces or slice and fry.
	Smoked.	Use as sandwich filling or blend with butter to make a cod's roe paste.
Herring	Hard roe, fresh uncooked.	Best fried in a little fat.
	Soft roe, fresh uncooked.	Either poach in milk or fry in butter.

Ready prepared fish

Kind of fish and how to buy		Best ways of cooking
Anchovies	Buy in cans, either flat fillets or rolled.	Add to sauces, use in salads, sandwiches.
Crab	Buy canned.	Use in salads and sandwiches.
Herrings	Buy fresh herrings canned.	Use in salads, sandwiches or for reheating.
Bismarcks or Rollmops	Buy in jars.	Use in salads.
Herring roes	Buy canned.	Generally heated and put on toast.
Lobster	Buy canned.	As crab.
Pilchards	Buy canned.	As herring.
Prawns, Shrimps	Buy frozen and allow to defrost at room temperature, or buy canned.	Use as fresh.
Salmon	Canned pink salmon is the cheaper quality, but quite suitable for cooked dishes. Red salmon is more expensive.	Use in salads, sandwich fillings or in dishes such as fish pie, fish cakes.
Sardines, Sild	Buy canned.	Use in salads, sandwich fillings, or serve on hot toast.
Tuna	Buy canned, either as portions or (more expensive) as fillets.	As salmon.

WAYS TO COOK FISH

There are several basic ways in which fish can be cooked:

BAKED FISH

Cooking time: see method

Oven temperature:
350–375°F., 180–190°C.,
Gas Mark 4–5

Serves 4

IMPERIAL · METRIC	AMERICAN
1–2 oz./25–50 g. butter or margarine	2–4 tablespoons butter or margarine
4 portions fish	4 portions fish
seasoning	seasoning
little lemon juice	little lemon juice

Spread half the butter or margarine over the baking dish. Put in the fish, thin fillets may be rolled or folded if wished. Season well and add a squeeze of lemon juice if not adding any other flavouring. Top with the rest of the butter or margarine. Bake in the centre of a moderate to moderately hot oven allowing the following times:
12–15 minutes for thin fillets of fish
15–20 minutes for rolled, folded or thick fillets of fish
20–25 minutes for whole small fish, thick slices or steaks

This method gives a brown top to the fish, rather like grilling, but if you wish to keep this soft and light, then either cover the fish with buttered foil or greaseproof paper, or put a lid on the dish or add several table- spoons milk or white wine. (This could be used as part of the liquid in a sauce to serve with the fish.)

The fillets of fish may be stuffed if wished (a veal stuffing, see page 48, is excellent). In this case allow another 5–10 minutes extra cooking time.

To stuff fillets Spread with the stuffing then roll firmly.

To stuff cutlets Press the stuffing against the cutlet and tie in position.

Flavourings for baked fish Put a thin layer of sliced tomatoes at the bottom of the buttered dish and over the top of the fish.

Put 2 oz. (50 g.; $\frac{1}{4}$ cup) finely chopped bacon at the bottom of the dish. Add the fish and top with more chopped bacon. Less butter or margarine will be needed.

STEAMED FISH

Cooking time: see method

Serves 1

IMPERIAL · METRIC	AMERICAN
1 portion fish	1 portion fish
seasoning	seasoning
$\frac{1}{2}$ oz./15 g. butter or margarine	1 tablespoon butter or margarine
1–2 tablespoons milk	1–3 tablespoons milk
Garnish	**Garnish**
parsley	parsley
lemon	lemon

As this method of cooking fish is rarely used except for invalid cooking it is doubtful whether you would be cooking more than one portion at a time.

Put the fish on to a buttered ovenproof plate large enough to fit over the top of a saucepan. Half fill the saucepan with water and bring this to the boil.

Season the fish, add a small knob of butter or margarine, and 1–2 tablespoons milk, then cover with a second plate, the lid of the saucepan or greased foil.

Place over the boiling water and cook for:
8–10 minutes for thin fillets of fish
10–12 minutes for folded, rolled or thicker fillets
12–15 minutes for whole fish

Lift the fish from the plate on to a clean but hot plate or dish, garnish with parsley and lemon or serve with a sauce.

This is an excellent way of cooking fish for small children. If one is not allowed to eat fat in any form, omit the butter and use skimmed milk (i.e. all cream removed). Dried non-fat milk is excellent in this case.

New fish dishes
There are various ways in which you may make fish interesting.
1 Try various methods of cooking, grilling and baking.
2 Try different sauces to serve with the fish.
3 Try new coatings on fish, for example in Scotland herrings are coated with oatmeal, rather than flour and then they are fried.
4 Add unusual flavours to the fish.

Bacon and tomato pudding (see page 46)

BOILED OR POACHED FISH

Cooking time: see method

IMPERIAL · METRIC
4 portions fish
salt
water
flavourings (optional, see below)

AMERICAN
4 portions fish
salt
water
flavorings (optional, see below)

Serves 4

While the term boiling fish is often used, that is incorrect as fish must *not* be boiled, it would break and the flavour be spoiled. It should be *poached*, i.e. cooked gently, allowing ½ pint (250 ml.; 1¼ cups) water, ½ level teaspoon salt to each portion of white fish. Omit the salt with smoked fish.

If cooking several pieces of fish, do not increase the amount of water a great deal; allow sufficient to cover the fish.

Put the fish into cold salted water, together with any flavouring, bring just to boiling point, lower the heat, simmer for:

3 minutes – thin fillets of fish
5 minutes – thicker fillets
7 minutes – thick slices or steaks
Lift the fish from the water, drain on the fish slice, then serve with butter and lemon or a sauce.

Flavourings for poached fish
Add a bouquet garni to the water. Make a fish stock by simmering the bones and skin of the fish, strain this and use in place of water. A few slices of lemon may be used, or the fish may be cooked in water with the addition of a small quantity of white wine.

GRILLED FISH

Cooking time: see method

IMPERIAL · METRIC
4 portions fish
1–2 oz./25–50 g. butter or margarine
seasoning
flavouring (optional, see below)

AMERICAN
4 portions fish
2–4 tablespoons butter or margarine
seasoning
flavoring (optional, see below)

Serves 4

Always heat the grill before putting fish under it as fish dries badly if cooked too slowly. Most fish will be cooked on the grid (rack) of the grill pan, so brush this with a little melted butter or margarine to prevent the fish sticking, or place the fish on a piece of greased aluminium foil. Put this on the grid or rack of the pan. Brush the fish with melted butter or margarine, season lightly. Grill for:
2–3 minutes for thin fillets of fish (These do not need turning.)
5 minutes for thicker fillets (These do not need turning

but lower the heat for last few minutes cooking time.) 9–10 minutes for thick slices or steaks (Turn the fish during cooking and brush second side with melted butter or margarine.)

Flavourings for grilled fish
Squeeze a little lemon juice over the fish with the seasoning. Blend finely grated lemon rind with the butter or use orange rind and juice for a change (particularly good with plaice). Add a pinch of curry powder to the melted butter (very good with cod).

BATTER FOR COATING FISH

Naturally you will not make a large quantity of batter to coat just one portion of fish. This is only worth doing if you have several pieces to coat.

IMPERIAL · METRIC
4 oz./100 g. flour
pinch salt
1 egg
12 tablespoons milk
½ oz./15 g. seasoned flour

AMERICAN
1 cup all-purpose flour
pinch salt
1 egg
1 cup milk
2 tablespoons seasoned flour

Sieve the flour with the salt, add the egg and beat well, then gradually beat in the milk. Milk and water could be used for a more economical coating, and for a thinner coating, use an extra 2 tablespoons milk.

Coat the fish with seasoned flour. Dip the fish into the batter. Lift out with a fork and spoon and hold

suspended over the batter so that any surplus may drop back into the bowl. This saves making any mess as you put the fish into the fat. It also avoids too thick a coating. Use the smaller amount of milk for solid pieces of fish such as cod, and the thinner batter i.e. the larger quantity of milk, for thinner pieces of fish.

FRIED FISH

Cooking time: see method

Serves 4

IMPERIAL · METRIC
4 portions fish
seasoning
coating
butter, fat or oil
Garnish
lemon
parsley

AMERICAN
4 portions fish
seasoning
coating
butter, shortening or oil
Garnish
lemon
parsley

There are two methods by which fish may be fried:
1 By frying in a small quantity of fat in a frying pan –
this method is called shallow frying.
2 By frying in a larger quantity of fat or oil in a pan,
known as deep frying.

Generally fish is coated for each method but it is
possible to fry fish without coating it if shallow frying.

To coat fish
In order to give a crisp brown coating to fish it needs
covering with flour, egg and breadcrumbs or batter.

Flour coating for fish
Allow 1–1½ oz. (25–40 g.; about ¼ cup) flour for four
good portions of fish, add a good pinch salt and shake
of pepper. Put the seasoned flour on a piece of greaseproof paper or on a flat dish.

Press the fish into the flour on one side, turn and
repeat on the second side. Lift on to a clean plate,
press the flour into the fish with a palette knife just
before frying.

Egg and breadcrumb coating for fish
Allow 1 egg, 2 oz. (50 g.; ½ cup) crisp breadcrumbs
(raspings) for four portions of fish plus ½–1 tablespoon
water.

In addition it is advisable to coat the fish in a little
flour before the egg and crumbs: the flour coating
makes certain the egg adheres to the fish.

First coat the fish with flour as above: then break
the egg on to a flat plate, add the water and mix
together with a fork. This makes the egg go further,
but it also gives a less thick coating.

Either put the fish into the egg and turn with two
knives or a spoon and fork, or brush the egg over the
fish by dipping a pastry brush into the beaten egg.

Put the crisp breadcrumbs either on to a flat plate
or a piece of greasproof paper or in a bag; with the
former turn the fish in the crumbs, with the bag drop
the fish into the crumbs and shake gently.

Lift from the crumbs, press these against the fish
which is then ready to fry.

To fry without coating
Dry the fish, season lightly. Heat 2–3 oz. (50–75 g.;
4–6 tablespoons) fat (in this method butter is often
used) in the frying pan. Heat gently and when hot but
not smoking, put in the fish, fry for the time given
below. Lift out on to a hot dish.

Continue heating any butter left in the pan until
golden brown in colour, add a teaspoon chopped

parsley and 1 teaspoon capers, if wished, with a
squeeze lemon juice. Pour over the fish. This method
is suitable for fillets of sole, trout and fresh haddock.

The name given to the dish when the butter is
allowed to become brown like this is *meunière*, so
sole cooked this way would be called *sole meunière*.

To shallow fry
Dry the fish very well after washing and coat in either
seasoned flour or egg and breadcrumbs. Heat approximately 2 oz. (50 g.; 4 tablespoons) fat (enough to give
a depth of a good ¼ inch; ½ cm.) for thin fish, or about
3 oz. (75 g.; 6 tablespoons) fat for thicker pieces of
fish. Test the temperature of the fat as when frying
fish in deep fat. Put in coated fish and cook for:
4 minutes for thin fillets of fish
(Turn after 2 minutes and cook for the same time on
the second side.)
5–6 minutes for thicker fillets
(Cook as above, then lower heat for final 1–2 minutes.)
7–9 minutes for thick pieces or whole fish
(Cook as thin fillets then lower heat for the final 3–5
minutes.)

To deep fry
A pan should be half filled with fat (lard or cooking fat)
or with oil (use olive or frying oil). Put the frying basket
into position when the fat or oil is hot. Meanwhile, coat
the dry fish with seasoned flour, then with egg and
crumb or batter coating. Test to see if the fat or oil
is sufficiently hot. A cube of bread should turn golden
brown within 1 minute in fat (oil takes slightly under
1 minute to brown the bread).

If the bread shows no signs of browning within this
time, heat the fat or oil longer and test again. If the
bread browns much more quickly, the fat or oil is too
hot. Remove pan from heat and cool, remember that
over-heated fat or oil can give an unpleasant taste.

Lower the fish carefully into the frying basket; never
bend over the pan of hot fat in case it splutters.

Reduce the heat slightly, so that the fat does not
continue to become hotter, cook for:
3 minutes for thin fillets of fish
4 minutes for thicker fillets of fish
5 minutes for thick pieces or steaks of fish

Lift the fish, in the frying basket, out of the pan of
hot fat, hold the basket over the pan for a few seconds
so surplus fat drains back into the pan.

Tip the fish on to absorbent paper on a hot plate or
tin. This drains off excess fat and makes sure the fish
is really crisp.

Testing fat

Coating fish in egg

Frying batter-coated fish in deep fat

Coating fish in breadcrumbs

Fried fish, a delicious meal

Fried fish in egg and breadcrumbs

SOUSED FISH

The most usual fish to cook in this way are herrings, mackerel and portions of cod, but other fish can be similarly treated.

Cooking time: 1 hour
Oven temperature:
300–325°F., 150–170°C.,
Gas Mark 2–3

Serves 4

IMPERIAL · METRIC
4 large or 8 small herrings or 4 mackerel
   or 4 portions white fish
1 teaspoon mixed pickling spice
1 teaspoon sugar
1 onion
¼ pint/125 ml. water
¼ pint/125 ml. vinegar
up to 1 teaspoon mixed spice or allspice
1–2 bay leaves

AMERICAN
4 large or 8 small herring or 4 mackerel
   or 4 portions white fish
1 teaspoon mixed pickling spice
1 teaspoon sugar
1 onion
⅔ cup water
⅔ cup vinegar
up to 1 teaspoon mixed spice or allspice
1–2 bay leaves

Split the fish and remove the backbone (see page 7). Roll so that you have the tail outside. Put into a shallow dish and add the rest of the ingredients, peeling and slicing the onion. Cover if wished and cook in the centre of a cool to moderate oven for about 1 hour.

This fish is generally served cold with salad but could be served hot if preferred. Some of the liquid can be added to mayonnaise if wished. To vary the flavouring of soused fish add 1–2 sliced apples; add a few gherkins or sliced cucumber when the fish is cooked.

SCALLOPS OF FISH FLORENTINE

Cooking time: 25 minutes
Oven temperature: 400°F.,
200°C., Gas Mark 5–6

Serves 4

IMPERIAL · METRIC
1 lb./½ kg. white fish
1 oz./25 g. butter
seasoning
lemon juice
1½–2 lb./¾–1 kg. spinach
½ pint/250 ml. white sauce, made with
   1½ oz./40 g. butter, 1½ oz./40 g. flour
   (page 50)
Topping
few browned breadcrumbs
1–2 oz./25–50 g. cheese, grated
little extra butter

AMERICAN
1 lb. white fish
2 tablespoons butter
seasoning
lemon juice
1½–2 lb. spinach
1¼ cups white sauce, made with
   3 tablespoons butter, 6 tablespoons
   all-purpose flour (page 50)
Topping
few dry bread crumbs
¼–½ cup grated cheese
little extra butter

Put the fish in a dish with the butter, seasoning and lemon juice, cover and bake in the oven until tender, about 15 minutes, or poach in seasoned water and lemon juice for 7–8 minutes. Prepare the spinach, cook, strain and sieve, place in buttered individual ovenproof dishes or scallop shells. Flake the fish into large pieces and arrange on the spinach. Make the

white sauce and spoon over the fish. Sprinkle with breadcrumbs and cheese, dot with small pieces of butter and brown under grill. Put each scallop shell on to a hot plate.
Note Use creamed potatoes instead of spinach, if preferred.

HALIBUT WITH GORGONZOLA

Cooking time: 10 minutes

Serves 2

IMPERIAL · METRIC
2 halibut steaks
4 oz./100 g. Gorgonzola cheese
1 oz./25 g. butter
2 tablespoons double cream
seasoning
Garnish
parsley

AMERICAN
2 halibut steaks
¼ lb. Gorgonzola cheese
2 tablespoons butter
3 tablespoons whipping cream
seasoning
Garnish
parsley

Place the halibut steaks in a grill pan (do not use the grid). Cream together the Gorgonzola cheese, butter and cream. Season to taste. Spread this mixture on one side of the halibut steaks and grill until cooked.

Garnish with parsley. Serve with hot mixed vegetables and/or salad.
Note Cheaper white fish – whiting or cod, may be used in place of halibut.

Halibut with Gorgonzola

Scallops of fish Florentine

BRETONNE FISH PIE

Cooking time: 30–35 minutes
Oven temperature:
425–450°F., 220–230°C.,
Gas Mark 7–8

Serves 6–8

IMPERIAL · METRIC
1 lb./½ kg. white fish, cod, fresh
  haddock, etc.
seasoning
6 oz./150 g. short crust pastry (page 64)

½ pint/250 ml. cheese sauce (page 51)
Garnish
6 canned asparagus tips
1–2 bacon rashers

AMERICAN
1 lb. white fish, cod, fresh haddock, etc.

seasoning
short crust pastry made with 1½ cups
  all-purpose flour, etc. (page 64)
1¼ cups cheese sauce (page 51)
Garnish
6 canned asparagus tips
1–2 bacon slices

Put the fish into cold water, add plenty of seasoning and simmer gently until tender, do not overcook. Make the pastry. Roll out and line a flan ring; if not available use a sandwich tin. Bake the pastry blind until crisp and golden brown (see page 65). Make the sauce, stir in the drained and flaked fish and put in the baked flan case. Top with the asparagus tips and the bacon rolled into small rolls and bake for approximately 10 minutes in the oven. Serve hot with vegetables or cold with salad.

FISH PUFFS

Cooking time: 3–4 minutes
for each batch

Serves 4

IMPERIAL · METRIC
8 oz./200 g. cooked fish
Batter
4 oz./100 g. plain flour
pinch salt
¼ pint/125 ml. water
1 tablespoon olive oil
1 tablespoon lemon juice
1 tablespoon capers
2 egg whites*
oil or fat for frying

AMERICAN
½ lb. cooked fish
Batter
1 cup all-purpose flour
pinch salt
⅔ cup water
1 tablespoon olive oil
1 tablespoon lemon juice
1 tablespoon capers
2 egg whites*
oil or shortening for frying

*Use the egg yolks in baked custard, see page 66.

Flake the cooked fish (this recipe is an ideal way to use left-over fish, or poach smoked or fresh white fish). Blend the flour, salt, water, oil and lemon juice. Add the chopped capers and fish. Lastly fold in the stiffly whipped egg whites. Heat a pan of oil or fat (see directions on page 32). Drop spoonfuls of the mixture into this and fry until crisp and golden, about 3–4 minutes. Lift out and drain on absorbent paper. Serve hot. These are excellent for a party snack or ideal, served with a sauce, for a main meal.

SUMMER FISH SALAD

Cooking time: 15–18 minutes

Serves 4

IMPERIAL · METRIC	AMERICAN
4 whiting	4 whiting
Dressing	**Dressing**
1 tablespoon olive oil	1 tablespoon olive oil
1 tablespoon lemon juice	1 tablespoon lemon juice
$\frac{1}{4}$ teaspoon paprika pepper	$\frac{1}{4}$ teaspoon paprika pepper
$\frac{3}{4}$ teaspoon mixed herbs	$\frac{3}{4}$ teaspoon mixed herbs
Garnish	**Garnish**
4 tomatoes	4 tomatoes
sliced cucumber	sliced cucumber
lettuce	lettuce

Grill the fish for 7–8 minutes on each side. Baste frequently with the dressing made from olive oil, lemon juice, paprika pepper and mixed herbs. Leave to cool, baste with the dressing to keep the fish moist. When cold, arrange on a serving platter on a bed of lettuce, garnish with tomatoes and slices of cucumber. Serve with bought or home-made mayonnaise (see page 53). **Note** Mackerel or herring may be cooked and served in the same way.

Cooking meat

The meat you can buy in this country is of first class quality; most other countries envy us for our high quality meat. Try and learn about the various cuts of meat, for they will enable you to shop well and economically.

On the following pages are the joints of meat and how they should be used.

Allow 8–12 oz. (200–300 g.) per person when buying meat on the bone, 6–8 oz. (150–200 g.) off bone, except for steak when 4–6 oz. (100–150 g.) can be allowed.

Beef

Cut	Ways of cooking
Aitchbone (Between top rump and top-side)	Roast if good quality. Boil, or pickle.
Bladebone	Stew or braise.
Brisket	Stew or braise. Pickle or boil. Slow roasting.
Clod	Stock for soups.
Fillet	Roast, grill or fry.
Flank	Stew or braise. Pickle or boil. Stock for soup.
Marrow bone	Stock for soup.
Neck	Stock for soup.
Oxtail	Stock for soup. Stew or braise.
Ribs	Roast.
Rump	Roast, grill or fry.
Shin or Leg	Stew, pickle or boil. Stock for soup.
Silverside	Pickle or boil.
Sirloin	Roast, grill or fry.
Skirt or Chuck	Stew or braise.
Topside	Roast or braise.

Lamb and mutton

Cut	Ways of cooking
Breast	Roast, stew, braise or boil.
Chops (From loin)	Grill or fry.
Cutlets	Grill or fry.
Head	Soup or stock. Use in brawn.
Leg (Divided into fillet of leg and shank end of leg)	Roast, stew, braise or boil.
Loin	Roast.

Cut	Ways of cooking
Best end of neck	Roast.
Middle neck	Stew, braise or boil.
Scrag end	Boil, soup or stock.
Saddle (A double loin)	Roast.
Shoulder	Roast, stew, braise or boil.
Trotters (Feet)	Soup or stock.

Pork

Cut	Ways of cooking
Belly	Boil.
Chops (From loin or spare rib)	Roast, fry or grill.
Head	Boil. Use in brawn.
Leg (Generally called knuckle of pork)	Roast, boil.
Loin	Roast, boil.
Spare rib	Roast, boil.
Trotters	Use for stews, brawn.

Veal

Cut	Ways of cooking
Breast	Roast, boil.
Chops (From loin)	Grill or fry.
Chump end of loin	Roast.
Feet	Boil, stock for soup.
Fillet	Roast, grill or fry. Stew or braise.
Knuckle	Stew or braise.
Leg	Grill or fry.
Thin leg slices	Grill.
Whole leg	Roast.
Loin	Roast.
Best end of neck	Roast.

Cut	Ways of cooking
Chops from best end	Grill or fry.
Middle and scrag end	Stew or braise.
Head	Boil. Use for brawn.

Offal

What to buy	How to use
Brains (Calf's, pig's, lamb's)	Wash well in cold water. Simmer in a little seasoned milk or water until tender, put into a white sauce.
Chitterlings (The small intestines of calf sold ready prepared by butchers)	Serve cold, or fry in a little hot fat.
Feet (Trotters, pig's, calf's, lamb's)	Generally used to make meat moulds or brawn because they contain a great deal of gelatine.
Faggots (Generally sold ready cooked by pork butchers)	Made from liver, kidney, belly of pork with crumbs and onion.
Head (Pig's, calf's, lamb's)	Generally used in brawn or can be served hot.
Heart (Pig's, calf's, lamb's)	When tender can be stuffed and roasted or braised.
Kidneys (Lamb's, calf's, pig's)	Fry or grill.
(Ox kidney)	Generally used in stewing, steak and kidney pie, or steak and kidney pudding.
Lights (Lungs of the animal)	Used for animal feeding only.
Liver (Pig's, lamb's, ox liver)	Fry or grill Braise
Pig's fry (Term given to a selection of offal from pig, including kidney and liver)	Fry or bake in oven.
Suet (Hard internal fat from mutton or ox)	Used in suet crust pastry puddings.
Sweetbreads (Lamb's or calf's come from the pancreas, throat and heart of the animal. Very easily digested. Fresh sweetbreads often difficult to obtain. Butchers now sell frozen sweetbreads)	First blanch by bringing to the boil in cold water. Throw away the water. Simmer for 25 minutes in salted water, skin, coat with egg and crumbs and fry or add to white sauce or braise.
Tail (Calf's or ox)	Generally braised.
Tongue	Often salted. May be boiled or pressed.
(Ox, calf's, pigs, lamb's)	Use in same way.
Tripe (From the stomach)	First blanch to whiten it. Bring to the boil, throw away water.

Bacon

It is important when choosing joints of bacon to make sure whether you have a sweet cure or mild cure, for these need no soaking. When bacon is well salted most people like joints soaked overnight in cold water before cooking. Here are some of the most usual cuts of bacon:

Cut	Ways of cooking
Back (Short or long cut into rashers)	Fry or grill.
(One piece)	Boil, bake or roast.
Collar (Fairly economical cut)	Boil or bake. Prime collar can be grilled or fried when cut into rashers.
Flank (Very economical cut)	Boil or bake.
Forehock (Fairly economical cut)	Boil or bake.
Gammon (Slipper, corner middle)	Grill, fry, bake, boil or roast.
Streaky (Economical rashers – top, prime, thin)	Grill or fry.

BOILED MEAT AND POULTRY

As pointed out under boiling fish, this is *not* the correct definition, meat should not be boiled rapidly, it should simmer steadily. If boiling salted meats (brisket, silverside of beef, tongue, bacon), soak them overnight, covered in cold water, next day remove from the water, discard this.

Put the fresh or soaked meat into a pan, add cold water to cover. Stir in a pinch of pepper and salt (with unsalted meats), together with vegetables if wished (onions, carrots). A bouquet garni may also be added.

Bring the water to the boil, there may be a thin slightly grey layer of bubbles and sediment on top, to keep liquid clear remove carefully with a spoon.

Cover the pan, lower the heat and cook for times given below:

Beef	30 minutes per lb. ($\frac{1}{2}$ kg.) and 30 minutes over; brisket can be given a little longer.
Lamb or Mutton	Often this will be lamb on the bone such as scrag end so allow a total cooking time of about $1\frac{1}{2}$ hours.
Bacon or Ham	Gammon about 20 minutes per lb. ($\frac{1}{2}$ kg.) and 20 minutes over, although thick cuts are better simmered gently for 25 minutes per lb. ($\frac{1}{2}$ kg.) and 25 minutes over. Cheaper joints, collar and forehock need minimum of 30 minutes per lb. ($\frac{1}{2}$ kg.) and 30 minutes over.
Tongue	About the same time as bacon.
Chicken	Good boiling fowl about 3 lb. ($1\frac{1}{2}$ kg.): 30 minutes per lb. ($\frac{1}{2}$ kg.) and 30 minutes over.

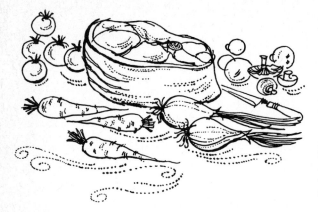

Accompaniments to boiled meat

Beef is served just with the vegetables and no sauce. Dumplings may be added (see page 45). Lamb or mutton is served with the vegetables and caper sauce.

Bacon or ham just with vegetables, or with parsley sauce (see page 51).

Tongue is skinned when tender, put into a tin so it forms a neat round. The liquid is boiled until a small quantity only is left. Dissolve 1 teaspoon gelatine in each $\frac{1}{2}$ pint (250 ml.; $1\frac{1}{4}$ cups) liquid, pour over the tongue, put a plate and light weight on top and leave until firm. Turn out and slice to serve cold with salad.

Chicken is served with a white, parsley or other sauce – made partially with milk and partially with chicken stock.

BAKED MEAT DISHES

Many meat dishes are baked, e.g. meat pies, shepherd's pie. Some people say that modern roasting is really baking because the meat is not cooked over or under an open fire on a spit. With some cookers there are spits supplied that turn under the grill and this produces the old conditions of roasting.

Glazed bacon (*Illustrated on page 22*)

Bacon may be glazed then baked for a short time in the oven.

Cook the bacon (see page 37) deducting approximately 30 minutes for the time it must be in the oven. Lift the bacon from water, cut away the skin from the fat. Make the glaze as follows:

Blend the grated rind of 1 or 2 lemons with the lemon juice and 3–4 tablespoons honey or blend 4–5 oz. (100–125 g.; about $\frac{1}{2}$ cup) brown sugar (demerara gives the best colour and texture) with 2 teaspoons made mustard and 4 tablespoons fruit syrup. Use peach, pineapple or apricot syrup, or fresh orange juice.

Spread or brush the glaze over the fat and bake for approximately 30 minutes in a moderately hot oven (375–400°F., 190–200°C., Gas Mark 5–6).

Note Canned, drained apricot halves and glacé cherries may be arranged on the bacon if wished, and garnished with watercress.

FRIED MEAT AND POULTRY

While meats may be cooked by deep frying it is easier to cook them in shallow fat.

Always choose tender meat for this purpose (see cuts on page 36).

The golden rule is to cook the meat fairly quickly on each side to seal in the flavour and juices, then to lower the heat and cook gently through to the centre.

Most fried meat can be served with fried tomatoes and mushrooms (see page 14).

Beef Choose cuts given in table. Heat 1–2 oz. (25–50 g.; 2–4 tablespoons) fat or butter in pan (enough for 4 steaks).

Underdone steak 2–3 minutes on each side except minute steak which needs just 1 minute on each side.
Medium rare About 4–5 minutes on each side.
Well done 5–6 minutes on each side.

Obviously, thickness determines time, the above times apply to steaks about $\frac{1}{2}$–$\frac{3}{4}$ inch (1–1$\frac{1}{2}$ cm.) thick.
Lamb Allow $\frac{1}{2}$–1 oz. (15–25 g.; 1–2 tablespoons) fat only. About 5–6 minutes each side.
Mutton If very tender as lamb.
Pork Add no fat, just grease pan, snip fat on pork itself to help it crisp. Allow 15–20 minutes.
Veal Coat with egg and crumbs or with flour as fish. Heat 2–3 oz. (50–75 g.; 4–6 tablespoons) butter or the equivalent in oil or fat, fry quickly for 2–3 minutes then lower heat, total cooking time about 15 minutes.
Bacon See breakfast dishes (page 14).
Chicken Always choose young frying chicken, coat as fish. Heat 2–3 oz. (50–75 g.; 4–6 tablespoons) fat or oil and cook quickly to brown, then lower heat to make sure chicken is cooked through. Total cooking time about 15 minutes.

GRILLED MEAT AND POULTRY

Always heat the grill before putting the meat under it. The one exception is slices of gammon when a very high starting heat causes the fat to curl badly.

Preparation and timing as frying, lower the heat after browning the outside or sealing the outside. Accompaniments as frying.

Brush the meat with melted butter or fat on each side to keep it moist.

For a change, serve grilled pork chops garnished with tomato baskets filled with peas, and with peeled apple slices brushed lightly with melted butter and grilled. (*Illustrated on the jacket.*)

Grilled gammon

Thick slices of grilled gammon (3$\frac{1}{2}$–4 minutes each side) may be served as part of the main meal. Remove the rind and snip the fat at regular intervals to prevent the slices from curling up.

For a special occasion, they can be garnished with lightly grilled pineapple and tomato baskets filled with peas. Arrange them on a dish, with peas in the centre, and serve with potato crisps.

Peach halves may be used instead of pineapple.

Apple rings, fried in hot bacon or pork fat until tender, are also a delicious accompaniment to grilled gammon.

ROAST MEAT AND POULTRY

It is important to select tender joints of meat for this method of cooking. If the meat has been frozen or is a cheaper cut it is advisable to choose the slower method of roasting.

Quick roasting

This means the meat is put into a hot oven (425–450°F., 220–230°C., Gas Mark 7–8) for the first 15 minutes if a very small joint, or up to 45 minutes for a joint of 5–6 lb. (2½–3 kg.) After this time the heat may be lowered to moderately hot (375–400°F., 190–200°C., Gas Mark 5–6).

Times to allow for quick roasting

Beef Underdone – 15 minutes per lb. (½ kg.) and 15 minutes over. Medium – 20 minutes per lb. (½ kg.) and 20 minutes over. Well done – as medium plus 10–15 minutes. Do not overcook beef since it becomes dry.
Lamb and mutton Most people like these meats well done so allow 20 minutes per lb. (½ kg.) for lamb and 20 minutes over and 25 minutes per lb. (½ kg.) for mutton and 25 minutes over (slower roasting, see below, is generally better for mutton).
Pork 25 minutes per lb. (½ kg.) and 25 minutes over.
Veal 25 minutes per lb. (½ kg.) and 25 minutes over.
Chicken, duck, turkey and goose 15 minutes per lb. (½ kg.) and 15 minutes over (if a turkey is over 12 lb. (6 kg.) add an extra 12 minutes only for each lb. (½ kg.) over this weight).
Note These times are suitable for joints over 3½–4 lb. (1¼–2 kg.); if a small joint add an extra 5–10 minutes to the *total* cooking time.*
Always weigh meat or poultry with the stuffing to calculate the cooking time.

*This means a joint of lamb at 2 lb. (1 kg.) needs 20 minutes per lb. (½ kg.) and 20 minutes over – 1 hour plus 5–10 minutes.

Slower roasting

The ideal heat for this is moderate (325–350°F., 170–180°C., Gas Mark 3–4) and it does make less expensive meat more tender.

Times to allow for slower roasting

Beef Underdone – 25 minutes per lb. (½ kg.) and 25 minutes over. Medium to well done – 35 minutes per lb. (½ kg.) and 25 minutes over.
Lamb and mutton 35 minutes per lb. (½ kg.) and 25 minutes over.
Pork and veal As for lamb.
Chicken and other poultry 25 minutes per lb. (½ kg.) and 25 minutes over; if the bird has been frozen then allow 30 minutes per lb. (½ kg.) and 30 minutes over.

See note about small joints and stuffing opposite. These times apply when using an ordinary open roasting pan.

OTHER METHODS OF ROASTING

Spit roasting

Many cookers today provide a turning spit and the meat therefore has even browning with a crisp outside. Times to allow – as quick roasting.

Foil roasting

The meat may be wrapped in aluminium foil to keep it moist (also to keep the oven clean).
Add an extra 15 minutes cooking time or 25°F. (10°C.) or 1 mark higher in the oven, since the heat has to penetrate through the foil. If the foil is only placed over the top of the roasting tin allow an extra 10 minutes. Remove the foil for the last 15–30 minutes, depending upon personal taste, to brown and crisp the meat.

Covered roasting tin

Make sure the meat does not fit too tightly in this, so there is space for the fat to splash and baste the meat, this gives browning, but for crispness the lid must be removed towards end of cooking, see foil roasting for extra time to allow.

BEST WAYS TO PREPARE AND COOK, AND ACCOMPANIMENTS TO SERVE WITH MEAT AND POULTRY

Beef Most cuts suitable for quick roasting but topside (particularly when chilled) or fresh brisket, better with slower roasting.
Choose Open pan, spit, foil or covered roasting pan.
Prepare Add about 1 oz. (25 g.; 2 tablespoons) fat only and just spread this over the lean part.
Serve with Yorkshire pudding, roast or new potatoes, other vegetables, thin gravy and mustard and/or horseradish cream.
Lamb Most cuts suitable for quick roasting though

slower roasting could be chosen if meat has been chilled or frozen.

Choose Open pan, spit, foil or covered roasting pan.

Prepare If very lean spread $\frac{1}{2}$–1 oz. (15–25 g.; 1–2 tablespoons) fat on lean parts.

Serve with Mint sauce or mint jelly, roast or new potatoes, thin gravy, other vegetables.

Mutton Generally better if roasted by slower method.

Choose As lamb.

Prepare As lamb.

Serve with Redcurrant jelly or onion sauce and thick or thin gravy according to personal taste.

Pork Suitable for quick or slow roasting according to personal taste.

Choose Open pan or spit roasting; do not cover if you want really crisp skin (crackling).

Prepare If the butcher has not scored i.e. marked the skin in cuts, do so as it helps it become crisp. Brush the fat with a little oil or melted lard or fat, sprinkled with a little salt if wished.

Serve with Apple sauce, sage and onion stuffing, thick gravy and vegetables.

Veal Suitable for quick or slow roasting according to personal taste.

Choose Preferably a covered roasting pan or foil to keep the meat moist, as it tends to become dry.

Prepare Either cover the veal with a generous amount of fat or streaky bacon or cut very thin strips of bacon fat, put them through a large needle (sold specially and called a larding needle) and thread through the meat. Add stuffing to the meat where possible to keep it moist. If using boned loin spread the stuffing on this, roll firmly and tie or skewer securely.

Serve with Veal stuffing (sometimes called parsley and lemon stuffing), sausages and/or bacon rolls, thick gravy and vegetables.

Chicken or turkey If not frozen, suitable for quick or slow roasting according to personal taste, frozen chicken and turkeys are better roasted by the slower method. (Make sure frozen poultry is completely thawed before cooking.)

Choose Open pan, spit roasting for chicken (a turkey is too big), foil or covered roaster.

Prepare Make stuffing (generally veal stuffing, but others may be used, see pages 48–50). Put into bird. Cover outside, especially the breast, with a little fat, butter, margarine or pieces of streaky bacon.

Serve with Veal stuffing, sausages, bacon rolls, bread sauce, thick gravy and vegetables.

Duck and goose If not frozen, suitable for quick or slow roasting according to personal taste; frozen duck and goose are better by the slower method.

Choose Open pan – too much fat flows from these birds to make them suitable for other methods and one needs to get a really crisp skin.

Prepare Add no fat, cook for 30 minutes, prick the skin gently, with a fine skewer or knitting needle, do this once more with a duck, twice more with a goose if possible (this allows the excess fat to escape during

cooking) – do not prick too deeply, otherwise the fat runs into the flesh.

With a goose it may be necessary to lift the bird out of the tin about three-quarters of the way through cooking and pour out the excess fat so the bird will become even more crisp-skinned. Sage and onion stuffing may be put into the bird or cooked separately. The latter is, I think, better, as the stuffing does tend to make the bird more greasy. Serve with sage and onion stuffing, apple sauce, thick gravy and vegetables.

A new look to roasted meat and poultry

Beef Sprinkle with a little dry mustard and flour before roasting; serve with a stuffing for a change.

Lamb Cut a clove of garlic into tiny slices and insert under the skin of the lamb. Boned breast of lamb (a very cheap and good cut but rather fat) can be spread with stuffing and rolled. Choose any stuffing in this book.

Mutton Arrange a thin layer of sliced raw onions and thickly sliced potatoes in the roasting pan, season. Cut away surplus fat from the mutton, so it does not make the vegetables too greasy, and roast in the usual way.

Pork Omit the apple sauce and sage and onion stuffing. Roast medium-sized raw onions in hot fat around the pork (these take 1 hour at the higher temperature), add cored, but not peeled, dessert apples about 40 minutes before the end of the cooking time.

Veal Stuff with sausage meat instead of the usual stuffing; 1–2 teaspoons freshly chopped mixed herbs (parsley, sage, thyme) and 2–3 rashers chopped bacon can be added to each 1 lb. ($\frac{1}{2}$ kg.) sausage meat.

Chicken or turkey Choose new stuffings for these.

Duck or goose Stuff with sliced peeled apples and/or soaked, but not cooked prunes. Both give an excellent flavour.

To use left-over cooked meat or poultry

This can be served cold with salads, used in dishes such as shepherd's pie (see page 43) or barbecued turkey pie (see opposite) – other meat or chicken can be used in place of turkey.

Favourite meat dishes

The preceding pages gave the ways to cook meat and the cuts to choose for various purposes. The recipes that follow are all prepared by these basic methods; several are very well known, others are more unusual, but I have selected all of these as being the kind of recipe you can vary, according to personal taste.

Baked meat and poultry dishes

The recipe for lamb pies is for a large number of small pies, as this is suitable for a party snack. Naturally, the quantities in the recipe may be reduced or the pies made larger for a family dish.

Barbecued turkey pie

BARBECUED TURKEY PIE

Cooking time: 55 minutes
Oven temperature:
375–400°F., 190–200°C.,
Gas Mark 5–6

Serves 4

IMPERIAL · METRIC
8 oz./200 g. short crust pastry (page 64)

Filling
1½–2 oz./40–50 g. lard
1 onion
1 8-oz./200-g. can tomatoes
1 2¼-oz./60-g. can tomato purée, or
    3 tablespoons
2 teaspoons paprika pepper
few drops Tabasco sauce
seasoning
squeeze lemon juice
2 teaspoons horseradish cream
1 tablespoon brown sugar
little stock, if necessary
12 oz.–1 lb./300 g.–½ kg. cooked turkey
1 egg to glaze

AMERICAN
short crust pastry made with 2 cups
    all-purpose flour etc. (page 64)

Filling
3–4 tablespoons lard
1 onion
1 8-oz. can tomatoes
¼ cup tomato paste

2 teaspoons paprika pepper
few drops Tabasco sauce
seasoning
squeeze lemon juice
2 teaspoons horseradish cream
1 tablespoon brown sugar
little stock, if necessary
¾–1 lb. cooked turkey
1 egg to glaze

Make the pastry. Melt the lard and cook the peeled and chopped onion gently until transparent. Pour off excess fat as the sauce should not be too greasy. Add the tomatoes from the can and the tomato purée, then add the other ingredients except the turkey, one by one, tasting between each addition so that the sauce suits individual palates. (These quantities give a sauce that is slightly hot, slightly sweet and slightly savoury, but proportions can be varied as liked.) Stir well after each addition and cook over a moderate heat. (This sauce can be made well in advance and kept, covered, in the refrigerator.)

Cut the turkey meat into large pieces. Put in a basin and mix with the sauce. This may be left in the pie dish, covered with foil, in the refrigerator for 24 hours until ready to bake. Roll out the pastry to cover, decorate with pastry trimmings and glaze with beaten egg. Bake in the middle of a moderately hot oven until golden brown – approximately 40 minutes.

Hot lamb pies

HOT LAMB PIES

Cooking time: about
45 minutes
Oven temperature: 425°F.,
220°C., Gas Mark 7

Makes 12 pies

IMPERIAL · METRIC	AMERICAN
1½ lb./¾ kg. lamb from leg or shoulder	1½ lb. boneless lamb, shoulder or leg
1 oz./25 g. fat or lamb dripping	2 tablespoons shortening or lamb drippings
1 10½-oz./265-g. can condensed mushroom soup	1 10½-oz. can condensed mushroom soup
seasoning	seasoning
1¼ lb./generous ½ kg. short crust pastry (page 64)	short crust pastry made with 5 cups all-purpose flour etc. (page 64)
1 egg to glaze	1 egg to glaze

Mince or chop the meat and fry in the hot fat or dripping until lightly browned. Stir in the soup and simmer gently for 15 minutes, until the meat is tender. Season to taste. Allow to become cold. Make the pastry, roll out and cut into twenty-four ¾-inch (1½-cm.) rounds or ovals, making twelve slightly larger for the tops. Divide the cold meat between the twelve smaller rounds or ovals. Damp the edges of the pastry and top with the second round or oval. Seal the edges and make a pattern around the edge, using either the point of a knife or a fork. Brush with beaten egg and bake in centre of a hot oven for about 25 minutes, until golden brown. Serve hot.

Note Make the pastry and filling the day before the party. Wrap the pastry in foil or polythene. Keep both in a cool larder or refrigerator. Remember to bring the pastry to room temperature before rolling it out. Bake on the day of the party. Heat before serving.

CORNISH PASTIES

Cooking time: 50 minutes
Oven temperature: 425°F.,
220°C., Gas Mark 7, reducing
to 350–375°F., 180–190°C.,
Gas Mark 4–5

Makes 2 large pasties

IMPERIAL · METRIC
8 oz./200 g. short crust pastry (page 64)

4–6 oz./100–150 g. uncooked rump steak
  or good quality stewing steak
1 large potato
1 large onion
good pinch salt
good shake pepper
1 tablespoon stock or water
milk or beaten egg to glaze

AMERICAN
short crust pastry made with 2 cups
  all-purpose flour etc. (page 64)
about ¼ lb. sirloin steak or good quality
  beef stew meat
1 large potato
1 large onion
good pinch salt
good shake pepper
1 tablespoon stock or water
milk or beaten egg to glaze

Make the short crust pastry and roll it into two rounds the size of a large tea plate. Cut the meat, the peeled potato and onion into ¼-inch (½-cm.) cubes and put on to a plate. Mix with the salt and pepper and put into the centre of each round of pastry. Add the stock or water to the meat mixture. Brush the edges of the pastry with a little water and press together lightly, so they will not open during cooking. Flute edges. Lift the pasties on to a lightly greased baking sheet, using a palette knife or fish slice. Brush with a little milk or beaten egg. Bake in the centre of a hot oven for 25 minutes, then lower the heat to moderate to moderately hot for a further 25 minutes to make sure the meat and vegetables are cooked. Serve hot or cold.

New look to meat pies

1 Use diced uncooked *young* chicken in place of steak in the Cornish pasty.
2 Use diced uncooked white fish in place of steak in the Cornish pasty.
3 Use diced cooked chicken or meat (veal is particularly good) in the barbecued turkey pie, see page 41).

SHEPHERD'S PIE

Cooking time: 1 hour
Oven temperature:
350–375°F., 180–190°C.,
Gas Mark 4–5

Serves 4

IMPERIAL · METRIC
1–1¼ lb./about ½ kg. potatoes, weight
  after peeling
seasoning
1½ oz./40 g. butter or margarine
8–12 oz./200–300 g. cooked meat
1 oz./25 g. dripping or fat
1 onion
2 tomatoes
good pinch mixed dried herbs
¼–½ pint/125–150 ml. brown sauce or clear
  brown stock or gravy*

AMERICAN
1–1¼ lb. potatoes, weight after peeling
seasoning
3 tablespoons butter or margarine
½–¾ lb. cooked meat
2 tablespoons drippings or shortening
1 onion
2 tomatoes
good pinch mixed dried herbs
⅔–1¼ cups brown sauce or clear brown
  stock or gravy*

*Gravy is a highly perishable food and even in a refrigerator it should not be stored for longer than 1–2 days.

Cook the potatoes in salted water until just soft. Drain, mash, add most of the butter or margarine and season well. Dice or mince the cooked meat. Heat the dripping or fat, fry the peeled and chopped onion and skinned, chopped tomatoes. Blend with the meat, herbs, sauce or stock or gravy and put into a pie dish. Top with the mashed potatoes, forking them into shape. Dot the rest of the butter or margarine on top which encourages the potato to brown. Bake for approximately 35 minutes just above the centre of a moderate to moderately hot oven.

New look to shepherd's pie

1 Use diced cooked poultry in place of meat.
2 Add a layer of sliced hard-boiled eggs over the top of the meat filling before covering with potato.
3 Use sliced cooked potatoes instead of mashed cooked potatoes.

MEAT AND POULTRY DISHES MADE BY BOILING AND STEWING METHODS

Although these dishes vary so much they are all cooked by boiling (or simmering) or stewing.

The stews may be cooked in a casserole in the centre of a very moderate oven. Use less liquid than in the recipe for you do not have as much evaporation as in a saucepan, i.e. if the recipe for a stew says 1 pint (500 ml.; 2½ cups) use ¾ pint (375 ml.; scant 2 cups) only.

MINCE COLLOPS

Cooking time: 1 hour

Serves 4

IMPERIAL · METRIC	AMERICAN
2 medium-sized onions	2 medium-sized onions
2–3 medium-sized tomatoes	2–3 medium-sized tomatoes
2 oz./50 g. fat	$\frac{1}{4}$ cup shortening
1 oz./25 g. flour	$\frac{1}{4}$ cup all-purpose flour
$\frac{1}{2}$ pint/250 ml. stock or use water and 1 beef stock cube	$1\frac{1}{4}$ cups stock or use water and 1 beef bouillon cube
1–1$\frac{1}{4}$ lb./about $\frac{1}{2}$ kg. minced beef	1–1$\frac{1}{4}$ lb. ground beef
seasoning	seasoning
good pinch mixed dried herbs, optional	good pinch mixed dried herbs, optional
Garnish	**Garnish**
2 slices bread	2 slices bread

Peel and chop the onions and tomatoes and cook steadily in the hot fat until the onions begin to soften, then work in the flour and cook gently for several minutes, stirring well. Gradually blend in the stock, or add the water and stock cube; bring to the boil and cook until thickened. Break up lumps of minced beef with a fork. Put into the sauce, continue to cook gently, stirring from time to time with a wooden spoon, for the meat still tends to form large lumps at the beginning of cooking. When well mixed add the seasoning and herbs. Put the lid on the pan and simmer for 45 minutes, stirring from time to time. If necessary, add a little more stock, but the mixture is better when fairly firm. Put on to a hot dish and garnish with triangles of toasted bread.

To give a new flavour to minced beef

1 Work 1 or 2 teaspoons curry powder into the onion and tomato mixture. Add the meat together with 1 oz. (25 g.; 3 tablespoons) sultanas, 2 teaspoons chutney, squeeze lemon juice and a pinch of sugar. Omit the herbs.

2 Omit the tomatoes and fry 2 oz. (50 g.; $\frac{1}{2}$ cup) sliced mushrooms with the onions.

3 Omit the flour, blend the stock into the fried onions and tomatoes, add the meat and continue as above. When the meat has cooked for 15 minutes stir in 1 oz. (25 g.; $\frac{1}{4}$ cup) rolled oats and continue cooking, stirring well from time to time. Season well.

4 Use minced mutton or lamb in place of beef, this may be flavoured with a little chopped mint; serve in a border of cooked peas.

To use left-over minced beef

Remember uncooked minced beef deteriorates quickly, due to the amount of cut surfaces, so use this soon after buying even when stored in a refrigerator. Reheat cooked minced beef thoroughly. Use in shepherd's pie if wished.

BEEF STEW WITH MIXED VEGETABLES

Cooking time: 2$\frac{1}{4}$–2$\frac{1}{2}$ hours

Serves 4

IMPERIAL · METRIC	AMERICAN
1–1$\frac{1}{2}$ lb./$\frac{1}{2}$–$\frac{3}{4}$ kg. beef steak, suitable for stewing	1–1$\frac{1}{2}$ lb. beef stew meat
2 oz./50 g. lard or cooking fat	$\frac{1}{4}$ cup lard or shortening
2 medium-sized onions	2 medium-sized onions
2 medium-sized carrots	2 medium-sized carrots
1 small turnip	1 small turnip
few sticks celery	few stalks celery
1$\frac{1}{2}$ pints water with 2 beef stock cubes or use brown stock	3$\frac{3}{4}$ cups water with 2 beef bouillon cubes or use brown stock
seasoning	seasoning
bouquet garni	bouquet garni
1 oz./25 g. flour	$\frac{1}{4}$ cup all-purpose flour

Cut the meat into neat pieces, remove any excess fat or gristle, but remember that a certain amount of fat gives flavour to the dish. Heat the lard or cooking fat in a large saucepan until melted, add the meat and turn in the fat for a few minutes. Peel and slice the onions, carrots and turnip neatly then blend with the meat in the fat. Chop the washed celery into pieces about 1 inch (2$\frac{1}{2}$ cm.) in length and add. Add 1$\frac{1}{4}$ pints ($\frac{3}{4}$ litre; generous 3 cups) of the water together with the crumbled stock cubes, or put in the stock. Bring just to boiling point, remove any grey bubbles (scum), see page 37. Add a little salt and pepper and the bouquet garni and cover the pan tightly. Simmer gently for 2 hours, or until the meat is just tender. Blend the flour with the rest of the stock or water, add to the stew stirring well. Cook until the liquid has thickened. Taste and add more seasoning if wished.

This is a basic stew, it can be varied in so many ways:

Add dumplings to the stew Make these as the recipe opposite. Thicken the stew as above and check carefully that there is plenty of liquid in the pan, for the dumplings absorb liquid very readily. Cook for 20 minutes in the gravy of the stew, which *should* boil steadily at this point and not simmer.

Make a beef cobbler Add a scone topping to the stew. When the stew is almost cooked, arrange unbaked scone rounds (use the recipe on page 75, but omit the sugar) on top of the stew; brush with milk and return to a very hot oven (450°F., 230°C., Gas Mark 8) for about 10 minutes to bake the scone topping. (*Illustrated on page 26*).

Use joints of chicken instead of beef. Jointed boiling fowl takes about 1½–2 hours; young chicken joints 1 hour.

Change the vegetables according to the season, e.g. add sliced green pepper (capsicum), beans, tomatoes and peas. (Where the vegetables cook quickly they should be put into the stew during cooking.)

Use lamb, mutton or veal See joints in table (page 36).

Add 1–2 teaspoons curry powder to the flour for a curry-flavoured stew.

DUMPLINGS

Cooking time: 20 minutes

Serves 4

IMPERIAL · METRIC
4 oz./100 g. self-raising flour

pinch salt
2 oz./50 g. shredded suet
water to mix (this varies from about
   2 tablespoons or a little more)

AMERICAN
1 cup all-purpose flour sifted with
   1 teaspoon baking powder
pinch salt
scant ½ cup finely chopped suet
water to mix (this varies from about
   3 tablespoons or a little more)

Sieve the flour and salt, add the suet and bind with the water. Form into eight small balls with floured hands. Do not have the dough *too stiff* otherwise the dumplings will not be as light as they should be. On the other hand, add the liquid gradually for if *too soft* they cannot be rolled into balls. Lower dumplings on top of the stew and cook until well risen.

New look to dumplings
1 Add ½–1 teaspoon chopped fresh herbs or a pinch of dried herbs.
2 Add 2–3 teaspoons grated onion, chopped spring onion or chives.
3 Add ½–1 tablespoon horseradish cream *before* adding the water.

STEAK AND KIDNEY PUDDING

Cooking time: 4 hours

Serves 4

IMPERIAL · METRIC
1 lb./½ kg. stewing steak
2 lamb's kidneys or 4 oz./100 g. ox kidney
2 teaspoons flour
¼ teaspoon salt
shake pepper
8 oz./200 g. suet crust pastry (page 64)

approximately ¼ pint/125 ml. water or
   stock

AMERICAN
1 lb. beef stew meat
2 lamb kidneys or ¼ lb. beef kidney
2 teaspoons flour
¼ teaspoon salt
shake pepper
suet crust pastry made with 2 cups
   all-purpose flour etc. (page 64)
about ⅔ cup water or stock

Trim the steak and cut into thin strips. Cut the kidney into small pieces. Either place a piece of kidney on each strip of steak and roll firmly, or mix the kidney and steak together. Either put the flour and seasoning on to a plate and toss the meat in this, or put the seasoned meat into the basin and sprinkle the flour between each layer. Make the pastry. There are two methods of lining the basin.

Method 1 Roll out nearly two-thirds of the pastry, lower into basin, pulling to avoid any uneven thick patches. Cut away any surplus pastry from top of basin, add to remaining pastry and use for the lid.

Method 2 Roll out all the pastry and form a round with this. Cut one-quarter of the round away, lower the large piece of pastry (with the piece removed) into the basin. Ease this together until the cut edges join, then press these together firmly. Cut away any surplus pastry from the top of the basin and add this to remaining pastry for the lid.

Put in the meat and add enough water or stock to come two-thirds of the way up the basin. Do not fill to the top otherwise the liquid will boil out. Roll out the remaining pastry to a round the size of the top of the basin, put this on top of the filled pudding. Cover with either greased paper, foil or a cloth dipped in boiling water and floured. Fix firmly round the basin rim. Put the pudding into a steamer, stand this over a saucepan of boiling water, making sure that it is balanced steadily. Steam for 4 hours. Allow the water to boil rapidly for the first 2 hours and add more boiling water when necessary.

Kent chicken pudding
Use 1 lb. (½ kg.) diced raw chicken with 12 oz. (300 g.) diced vegetables in place of steak and kidney.

New look to meat puddings
1 Omit the kidneys in the steak and kidney pudding

and add sliced onion and/or sliced mushrooms. Vary the amount according to personal taste.

2 Use diced loin of lamb instead of the chicken or beef in either of the puddings.

3 Use chopped bacon and tomatoes in place of the steak and kidney. Add some diced carrot and chopped onion. Garnish with watercress.
(*Illustrated on page 30*).

MEAT DISHES USING THE GRILL OR FRYING PAN

SAUSAGE CAKES

Cooking time: 15 minutes

Serves 4–6*

IMPERIAL · METRIC
8 oz./200 g. cooked mashed potatoes
   (page 58) or 1 small packet potato
   powder** prepared as directed
1 small onion
½ oz./15 g. fat
8 oz./200 g. beef or pork sausage meat
Coating
1 egg
1 oz./25 g. crisp breadcrumbs
2 oz./50 g. fat for frying
Garnish
parsley

AMERICAN
½ lb. cooked mashed potatoes (page 58)
   or 1 small package potato powder**
   prepared as directed
1 small onion
1 tablespoon shortening
½ lb. beef or pork sausage meat
Coating
1 egg
¼ cup dry bread crumbs
¼ cup shortening for frying
Garnish
parsley

*Will serve up to six if served with rashers of bacon or fried eggs.
**If very soft you will need to add ½ oz. (15 g.; 2 tablespoons) flour to stiffen the mixture.

Put the potatoes into a large saucepan and reheat gently, this makes it easier to mix with the sausage meat. Meanwhile chop the peeled onion finely. Heat the fat and toss the onion in this until just soft, add potatoes and onion to the sausage meat, blend well.

Form into four large, six medium or eight small round flat cakes with your hands and a flat bladed palette knife. Brush each cake with beaten egg and coat with the crisp breadcrumbs – this can be done with the crumbs on a large plate or large sheet of greaseproof paper or by putting the crumbs into a large paper bag, dropping the cakes in this and shaking firmly until evenly coated. Lift the cakes from the crumbs, pat into a perfect shape again with the palette knife – this also presses any loose crumbs against the cakes. Heat the fat in the pan and fry the cakes quickly on each side until crisp and golden brown. Lower the heat and cook gently for 10 minutes to make sure sausage meat is cooked. Drain on absorbent paper for 1 minute then serve garnished with parsley.

FRIED CHICKEN IN SAVOURY RICE RING

Cooking time: 35 minutes

Serves 4

IMPERIAL · METRIC
1 frying chicken
1 oz./25 g. flour
seasoning
3 oz./75 g. lard
6 oz./150 g. long-grain rice
1 11-oz./275-g. can sweetcorn
1 small packet frozen peas and carrots
Sauce
1½ oz./40 g. butter
1½ oz./40 g. flour
½ pint/250 ml. milk
¼ pint/125 ml. chicken stock*
3 tablespoons double cream
Garnish
chopped parsley

AMERICAN
1 frying chicken
¼ cup all-purpose flour
seasoning
6 tablespoons lard
scant 1 cup long-grain rice
1 11-oz. can kernel corn
1 small package frozen peas and carrots
Sauce
3 tablespoons butter
6 tablespoons all-purpose flour
1¼ cups milk
⅔ cup chicken stock*
scant ¼ cup whipping cream
Garnish
chopped parsley

*Made by simmering the giblets.

Cut the chicken into neat pieces and coat in the flour mixed with seasoning. Fry steadily in the hot lard until golden brown, approximately 15 minutes. Meanwhile boil the rice in 1 pint (500 ml.; 2½ cups) salted water for 15 minutes, adding the corn and frozen vegetables after 10 minutes and seasoning well. Make the sauce (see page 50) using the milk and chicken stock (if no chicken stock is available then use water and ½ chicken stock cube). When the sauce is thick blend in the cream. Put the rice mixture into a ring mould for a few minutes, standing this in a warm place.

Turn out on to hot serving dish. Fill centre with fried chicken, coat with the sauce and garnish with chopped parsley.

46

RUMP STEAK MELBOURNE

Cook rump steak under a heated grill and garnish with tomatoes and mushrooms and serve with parsley butter. This dish is as popular in Australia as it is here.

PARSLEY OR MAITRE D'HOTEL BUTTER

Serves 4

IMPERIAL · METRIC	AMERICAN
2 oz./50 g. butter	$\frac{1}{4}$ cup butter
1 teaspoon lemon juice	1 teaspoon lemon juice
2–3 teaspoons chopped parsley	2–3 teaspoons chopped parsley

Cream the butter with the lemon juice. Add the parsley. Form into four neat shapes and chill these if possible. Put on the steak just before serving.

Rump steak Melbourne

SWEDISH MEAT BALL PIE

Cooking time: 40 minutes
Oven temperature: 375°F.,
190°C., Gas Mark 5

Serves 4

IMPERIAL · METRIC	AMERICAN
1 lb./½ kg. rump steak	1 lb. rump steak
1 egg	1 egg
½ oz./15 g. fresh breadcrumbs	¼ cup fresh soft bread crumbs
½ teaspoon salt	½ teaspoon salt
pinch pepper	pinch pepper
pinch grated nutmeg	pinch grated nutmeg
¼ pint plus 5 tablespoons/225 ml. milk	⅔ cup plus 6 tablespoons milk
1 onion	1 onion
4 tablespoons oil	⅓ cup oil
2 tomatoes	2 tomatoes
½ oz./15 g. cornflour or 1 oz./25 g. flour	2 tablespoons cornstarch or ¼ cup all-purpose flour
1 beef stock cube	1 beef bouillon cube
¾ pint/375 ml. boiling water	scant 2 cups boiling water
1 tablespoon tomato purée	1 tablespoon tomato paste
1½–2 lb./¾–1 kg. potatoes, cooked and mashed	1½–2 lb. potatoes, cooked and mashed
Garnish	**Garnish**
2 tomatoes	2 tomatoes
little parsley	little parsley

Mince or chop the meat finely. Mix with the beaten egg, breadcrumbs, seasoning and nutmeg. Bind the ingredients together with the milk. Form into small balls. Peel and chop the onion finely and fry in the oil in a frying pan, then put in a casserole with the sliced, skinned tomatoes. Add the cornflour or flour to the remainder of the oil in the pan. Cook for 1 minute, stirring well. Blend in the stock (made by dissolving the beef cube in the boiling water) and tomato purée. Bring to boil and cook for 1 minute stirring constantly. Pour the sauce over the meat balls in casserole and pipe or spread the mashed potato over the top or around the edge. Bake for 30 minutes just above centre of a moderately hot oven. Garnish with sliced tomato and parsley.

MEAT AND POULTRY DISHES THAT ARE ROASTED

The basic instructions for roasted meat and poultry should be followed (see pages 39–40); the dish is given quite a variation in flavour by stuffings and sauces.

The sauces mentioned will be found in the next section; this also gives a recipe for gravy.

Stuffing recipes follow, but remember when in a hurry you can buy packets of prepared stuffings.

You can give these an individual flavour with extra chopped herbs, or by using the recipe below.

CORN AND APRICOT STUFFING

Blend a packet of sage and onion or veal stuffing with the drained contents of a can of corn; do *not* use creamed corn. Bind with some of the syrup from a small can of apricots which can be used as a garnish, heating these in the syrup.

This is a favourite stuffing in Australia where apricots are so magnificent.

VEAL STUFFING

This is also known as lemon and parsley stuffing.

Serves 4–6

IMPERIAL · METRIC	AMERICAN
2 oz./50 g. shredded suet or melted butter or margarine	scant ½ cup finely chopped suet or ¼ cup melted butter or margarine
½ teaspoon mixed dried or 1 teaspoon fresh chopped herbs	½ teaspoon mixed dried herbs or 1 teaspoon fresh chopped herbs
grated rind and juice of ½ lemon	grated rind and juice of ½ lemon
4 oz./100 g. breadcrumbs	2 cups fresh soft bread crumbs
1 egg	1 egg
seasoning	seasoning
2–4 teaspoons chopped parsley	2–4 teaspoons chopped parsley

Mix all the ingredients together. If wished, a little stock or milk may be added to give a soft stuffing. This is the most popular stuffing of all and can be used with meat, fish, poultry and vegetables. The cooked giblets or cooked liver from poultry can be chopped finely and added if wished.

Coleslaw served with slices of ham (see page 59)

SAGE AND ONION STUFFING

Cooking time: 10–20 minutes, plus time in the oven

Serves 4

IMPERIAL · METRIC	AMERICAN
2–3 large onions	2–3 large onions
½ pint/250 ml. water	1¼ cups water
seasoning	seasoning
3–4 oz./75–100 g. breadcrumbs	1½–2 cups fresh soft bread crumbs
1–2 teaspoons dried or chopped fresh sage	1–2 teaspoons dried or chopped fresh sage
1 egg (optional)	1 egg (optional)

Peel the onions, chop if wishing to shorten cooking time. Put into the water, add seasoning and cook until moderately soft. Lift out of the water, chop then add to the rest of the ingredients. Bind with egg or onion stock. Use for stuffing pork and duck.

To make sauces

A good sauce is a matter of careful blending of ingredients, stirring well as the sauce thickens and tasting to make certain that it is well, but not over-seasoned. Gravy is one type of sauce so is included in this section.

To prevent a skin forming while the sauce is kept waiting: when the sauce has thickened, place a piece of really damp greaseproof paper or foil into the saucepan so that it just rests above the sauce, then no skin will form.

Another way of preventing this is to use almost all the liquid, make the sauce, pour the remainder of the liquid over the top. When reheating the sauce, either remove the paper carefully if using method 1, or stir in the extra liquid with method 2.

Making a white sauce

A white sauce is the basis for many other flavoured sauces. It is an excellent way to add milk to the diet, and at the same time it can be used in many different ways.

There are two basic methods of making a sauce. They are both given here and give a coating consistency – the first method is the easier of the two.

WHITE SAUCE 1
(BLENDING METHOD)

Cooking time: 10 minutes

Serves 2–4*

IMPERIAL · METRIC	AMERICAN
1 oz./25 g. flour	¼ cup all-purpose flour
pinch salt	pinch salt
shake pepper	shake pepper
½ pint/generous ¼ litre milk	1¼ cups milk
½–1 oz./15–25 g. butter or margarine	1–2 tablespoons butter or margarine

*Dependent upon way it is used – will serve 4 as coating on vegetables, 2 as part of main dish.

Blend the flour with the seasoning and a quarter of the milk in a basin, stirring to a smooth paste with a wooden spoon. Bring the rest of the milk to the boil, pour slowly over the flour mixture, stirring all the time to prevent lumps forming. Tip the sauce back into the saucepan, stir over a low heat until the mixture boils, and cook for 3 minutes stirring all the time. Add the butter or margarine towards the end of the time. Taste, and if necessary, add more salt and pepper.

WHITE SAUCE 2
(ROUX METHOD)

Cooking time: 10 minutes

Serves 2–4

IMPERIAL · METRIC	AMERICAN
1 oz./25 g. butter or margarine	2 tablespoons butter or margarine
1 oz./25 g. flour	¼ cup all-purpose flour
½ pint/generous ¼ litre milk	1¼ cups milk
pinch salt	pinch salt
shake pepper	shake pepper

Melt the butter or margarine in a small saucepan. Remove from the heat, stir in the flour with a wooden spoon. Return this mixture of fat and flour – called the roux – to a low heat and cook for 2–3 minutes, stirring well; take care that the roux does not change colour, cook only until it is dry and crumbly. Remove the pan from the heat once again, gradually stir in the milk (or milk and vegetable or meat stock, see variations on white sauce, opposite). Add the liquid sufficiently slowly so it blends into the roux and the mixture remains smooth. Add the salt and pepper and put the sauce back over the heat and bring to the boil, stirring all the time. When the sauce has come to the boil, lower the heat and continue cooking for 3 minutes. Taste and, if necessary, add more salt and pepper.

Sauces based on white sauce

To serve with vegetables – Basic recipe but use half milk and half vegetable stock; this gives a better flavour and uses the valuable vitamins in the vegetable stock.

Cheese sauce To serve with fish, vegetables, macaroni. Basic recipe, adding pinch of dry mustard to the flour. When cooked, stir in 2–4 oz. (50–100 g.; $\frac{1}{2}$–1 cup) finely grated Cheddar cheese, cook for 1 minute only over a low heat until cheese has melted.

Mustard sauce To serve with fish, particularly herrings. Recipe 1 (blending method) but add $\frac{1}{2}$–1 teaspoon dry mustard with flour.

Mushroom sauce To serve with fish, egg or meat dishes. Wash and chop 1–2 oz. (25–50 g.; about $\frac{1}{2}$ cup) mushrooms, simmer in $\frac{1}{2}$ pint (250 ml.; 1$\frac{1}{4}$ cups) milk for 5 minutes. Make the roux of the butter or margarine and flour (white sauce 2), in another saucepan, then gradually blend in the milk and mushrooms, cook as before. Season well.

Parsley sauce To serve with vegetables, fish or bacon. Basic recipe. Use all milk or for boiled bacon use half milk and half bacon stock. When cooked add 2–3 teaspoons finely chopped parsley.

To vary the consistency of white and similar sauces adjust the proportions of liquid, e.g. a thin white sauce is made as the coating consistency (see page 50) but use 1 pint (generous $\frac{1}{2}$ litre; 2$\frac{1}{2}$ cups) milk. This is used to add to vegetable purées in soup (see page 24).

A thick white sauce, often called a panada, is made as the coating consistency (see page 50) but use $\frac{1}{4}$ pint (125 ml.; $\frac{2}{3}$ cup) milk. This is used to bind ingredients together.

BROWN SAUCE

Cooking time: 10 minutes

Serves 2–4

IMPERIAL · METRIC	AMERICAN
1 oz./25 g. dripping or fat	2 tablespoons drippings or shortening
1 oz./25 g. flour	$\frac{1}{4}$ cup all-purpose flour
$\frac{1}{2}$ pint/250 ml. brown stock or water and 1 beef stock cube	1$\frac{1}{4}$ cups brown stock or water and 1 beef bouillon cube

Follow the directions for white sauce on page 50 using either method, i.e. blending or roux.

GRAVY

Pour or spoon away all surplus fat, except 1 tablespoon, from the roasting pan. Either make the gravy in the roasting pan or pour this into a saucepan (use any pieces of meat or stuffing – generally called the sediment – as this adds flavour).

Thin gravy Blend 1 tablespoon gravy powder (which acts as flavouring and thickening) into the dripping in the pan or use just under 1 tablespoon flour and 1 teaspoon gravy powder or add a little vegetable or beef extract to taste.

Thick gravy Use up to double the ingredients for the thin gravy above.

Cook the flour for 1 minute in the dripping, stirring well. Gradually blend in $\frac{1}{2}$ pint (generous $\frac{1}{4}$ litre; 1$\frac{1}{4}$ cups) of liquid. This can be brown stock, or most people use the liquid from cooking vegetables so that they use the vitamins and mineral salts that are in this liquid. Cook as for white sauce (see page 50) until thickened; taste, add extra seasoning if wished and strain into a hot sauceboat.

BREAD SAUCE

Cooking time: few minutes, plus time to infuse

Serves 4

IMPERIAL · METRIC	AMERICAN
1 small onion	1 small onion
2 or 3 cloves (optional)	2 or 3 cloves (optional)
$\frac{1}{2}$ pint/250 ml. milk	1$\frac{1}{4}$ cups milk
2 oz./50 g. breadcrumbs	1 cup fresh soft bread crumbs
1–2 oz./25–50 g. butter or margarine	2–4 tablespoons butter or margarine
salt and pepper	salt and pepper

Peel the onion. If using cloves, stick them firmly into it. Put the onion into the milk together with the other ingredients. Slowly bring the milk to the boil. Remove from the heat and leave in a warm place for as long as possible – this makes sure the milk absorbs the flavour.

Just before the meal is ready, remove the onion, heat the sauce gently, beating it with a wooden spoon.

Put into a sauceboat.

Note Bread sauce is inclined to burn at the bottom of the pan unless it is stirred very carefully. You may have interruptions when you are busy cooking a complete meal and it is a good idea to prepare the bread sauce and put this over hot water, i.e. either in a basin covered with foil, or the top of double saucepan over a pan of hot water.

Apple and nut salad (see page 61)

APPLE SAUCE

Cooking time: 15 minutes

Serves 4–6

IMPERIAL · METRIC
1 lb./½ kg. cooking apples
¼ pint/125 ml. water
1–2 oz./25–50 g. sugar
1 oz./25 g. butter (optional)

AMERICAN
1 lb. baking apples
⅔ cup water
2–4 tablespoons sugar
2 tablespoons butter (optional)

Peel the apples, core, slice and cook with the water and sugar until a soft purée. Add the butter if wished. Either sieve, beat with a wooden spoon or put into a warmed blender until smooth. If the sauce is a little thin (for some apples are juicier than others) remove the lid and boil fairly quickly to evaporate some of the moisture.

SAVOURY SALAD DRESSING

Serves 4

IMPERIAL · METRIC
1 carton natural yoghourt
1 tablespoon finely chopped spring onion
  or chives
½ teaspoon made mustard
1 teaspoon chopped parsley
seasoning
pinch sugar
squeeze lemon juice

AMERICAN
1 carton unflavored yogurt
1 tablespoon finely chopped scallion
  or chives
½ teaspoon made mustard
1 teaspoon chopped parsley
seasoning
pinch sugar
squeeze lemon juice

Blend all the ingredients together.

BOLOGNESE SAUCE

Cooking time: 2–2½ hours

Serves 4

IMPERIAL · METRIC
2 medium-sized onions
2 oz./50 g. butter
1 lb./½ kg. minced beef
1 clove garlic (optional)
2 tablespoons tomato purée
8 oz./200 g. tomatoes, skinned and
  de-seeded*
seasoning
¼ pint/125 ml. water

AMERICAN
2 medium-sized onions
¼ cup butter
1 lb. ground beef
1 clove garlic (optional)
3 tablespoons tomato paste
½ lb. tomatoes, skinned and de-seeded*

seasoning
⅔ cup water

*To skin tomatoes, see page 55. To de-seed tomatoes, halve and scoop out the seeds with a teaspoon.

Peel the onions and chop fairly finely. Heat the butter. Lightly brown the onions in the butter, add beef and crushed garlic; cook for 5 minutes, stirring well. Add the tomato purée, tomatoes, seasoning and water; cover the pan and simmer for 1½–2 hours.

HOME-MADE MAYONNAISE

Serves 4

IMPERIAL · METRIC
1 egg yolk
good pinch salt
good pinch pepper
pinch mustard
4–8 tablespoons olive oil
2 teaspoons vinegar
2 teaspoons warm water

AMERICAN
1 egg yolk
good pinch salt
good pinch pepper
pinch mustard
⅓–⅔ cup olive oil
2 teaspoons vinegar
2 teaspoons warm water

Put egg yolk and seasonings into a basin. Gradually beat in the oil, drop by drop, stirring until mixture is thick. Beat in vinegar gradually, then the warm water.

Cream cheese mayonnaise
Blend 2 oz. (50 g.; ¼ cup) cream cheese gradually into about 6 tablespoons (½ cup) mayonnaise – this is excellent with a mixed vegetable or potato salad.

A new look to mayonnaise
Home-made or ready prepared mayonnaise may be given a new flavour by:
1 Adding a little tomato ketchup or tomato purée.
2. Adding 1–2 teaspoons chopped parsley, 1–2 teaspoons chopped gherkins, and 1–2 teaspoons capers, to each ¼ pint (125 ml.; ⅔ cup) mayonnaise to make tartare sauce.

QUICK TOMATO SAUCE

Cooking time: 15–20 minutes

Serves 4–5

IMPERIAL · METRIC
1½ oz./40 g. butter
1 small onion
1 small apple
1 small tube or can tomato purée
2 teaspoons cornflour
¾ pint/375 ml. water
seasoning
good pinch sugar (optional)

AMERICAN
3 tablespoons butter
1 small onion
1 small apple
¼ cup tomato paste
2 teaspoons cornstarch
scant 2 cups water
seasoning
good pinch sugar (optional)

Heat the butter and fry the peeled and chopped onion for a few minutes, then fry the grated, peeled apple. Add the purée and the cornflour blended with the water and seasoning. Bring to the boil and stir until smooth. Simmer gently for about 10 minutes, taste and re-season, adding sugar if wished.

This sauce may be varied by adding chopped cooked ham, chopped olives, or using a large can of tomatoes and the liquid from these instead of tomato purée and water.

FRENCH DRESSING

Serves 4

IMPERIAL · METRIC
½–1 teaspoon made or French mustard
good pinch salt
good shake pepper
pinch sugar
3–4 tablespoons salad or olive oil
1½–2 tablespoons vinegar or lemon juice

AMERICAN
½–1 teaspoon made or French mustard
good pinch salt
good shake pepper
pinch sugar
¼–⅓ cup salad or olive oil
2–3 tablespoons vinegar or lemon juice

Put the mustard, seasoning and sugar into a basin, blend in the oil gradually, then the vinegar or lemon juice. Or put the ingredients into a screw-topped jar and shake hard until mixed or put into electric blender.

The proportion of oil and vinegar may be varied according to personal taste; chopped herbs, crushed garlic may be added. A larger quantity may be made and stored in a screw-topped jar. Shake before using.

READY MADE SAUCES

There are many dehydrated sauce mixes available which are simple to prepare.
Ready prepared mayonnaise This may be warmed in a basin over hot water and used as a savoury sauce.
Concentrated or condensed soups These may be heated undiluted as a sauce.

Salads and vegetables

A green salad
To be strictly correct a green salad should consist of lettuce, watercress, cucumber, green pepper and chicory, but should not have other ingredients such as tomatoes, eggs, radishes. The ingredients should be prepared and tossed in a dressing just before serving. However, it may be prepared and arranged and people left to add their own dressing as required.

A classic mixed salad consists of all the ingredients above when available, plus hard-boiled eggs, tomatoes and radishes – fruit may be added if required (see salad suggestions on page 59).

TO CHOOSE AND PREPARE INGREDIENTS FOR SALADS

Beetroot See vegetables.
Celery and chicory Good celery should have firm pale green leaves, good chicory should be white and firm.
To prepare Pull away the stalks from the celery and wash in plenty of cold water. Trim chicory and wash in cold water. Either vegetable may be diced or cut into portions. If thin strips of celery are put into iced water and left for 1–2 hours they form attractive curls.
Cucumber A good cucumber is firm and rigid, if limp it is stale.
To prepare Wipe the skin unless you are peeling the cucumber. Cut into wafer-thin slices, put on to a plate or shallow dish, add a little salt, pepper and vinegar. To give an attractive effect to the peel, score the skin by dragging the point of a fork down very firmly.
Lettuce or endive In Britain endive is a rather curly looking lettuce, in France and the U.S.A. it is a white vegetable we know as chicory. The first must be firm and green. Feel the heart gently and it should be fairly solid.
To prepare Wash carefully, pull the leaves apart, either dry by shaking in a salad shaker or strain away surplus moisture and put on to a folded tea towel and press gently. When dry, either serve the separate leaves or shred the leaves. Use a silver or stainless steel knife to prevent discoloration.

Cabbage and other green vegetables used in cole-slaw should be fresh, firm and green and washed carefully.

Radishes These should be quite firm. Do not worry unduly if the leaves look a little dead for they die very quickly but the radish, edible part, will still remain in good condition.

To prepare Remove stalk, wash, dry and either slice or cut into water lilies as for tomatoes, or with practice you can make more elaborate shapes by cutting the actual skin away from the centre of the radish in petal shapes. If time permits though, the easiest way to make a flower is to cut the radish from the top into about eight sections. Do not cut right down to the bottom. Put into very cold water for an hour or so and these will open up.

Spring onions Watch that these are not slimy, if they are they are very unpleasant.

To prepare Remove outer skin and roots, cut away surplus green tips, wash and dry well.

Tomatoes Check that these are firm, unbruised and yet ripe.

To prepare Skin by lowering carefully into hot water for a minute and then into cold water, slice or cut into portions. If the skin is left on, cut into water lily shapes. To do this use a sharp knife. Insert the point of the knife into the tomato and cut into a Vandyke fashion through the tomato, each time feeling the point of the knife going through to the centre. When you have completed doing this pull the tomato gently apart and you have two halves forming water lily shapes.

Watercress and mustard and cress These should look firm and green and not limp.

To prepare watercress Cut or peel the top sprigs from the stalks. Wash as lettuce.

To prepare mustard and cress Use a small amount at a time. Cut away from the roots with scissors, hold between finger and thumb, wash, discard seeds.

TO CHOOSE AND PREPARE VEGETABLES

Artichokes, globe Must be green and firm, not wrinkled.

To prepare Cook steadily in boiling salted water for about 30 minutes. Serve with a little melted butter.

Artichokes, Jerusalem Should be firm without any bruised parts.

To prepare Scrub well and peel or scrape. Soak in a little cold water, adding a few drops of vinegar. Cook for about 30 minutes in boiling water adding a few drops of vinegar. Serve with melted butter, white, cheese or Hollandaise sauce.

Asparagus and cheese sauce

Fruit salad (see page 70)

Asparagus Must be firm and green, if limp it is stale.
To prepare Wash carefully, then cut off a little of the thick white base of stalks. Either steam or boil the bunch in salted water in a tall pan for 20–25 minutes. Serve with melted butter, mousseline or cheese sauce.
Beans, broad Should be pale green and flexible.
To prepare Shell and wash, unless very young, when they can be cooked whole. Cook in boiling salted water for about 20 minutes. Serve with a little melted butter and chopped parsley.
Beans, French or runner Should be flexible; old beans cannot be bent, they will break.
To prepare Wash and string. French beans can be left whole, but runner beans are better thinly sliced. Cook steadily in boiling salted water for about 15 minutes. Toss in a little butter or margarine.
Beetroot If cooked should never be slimy.
To prepare Wash carefully and cook in boiling salted water until soft; time will vary according to size, but test by pressing gently. Skin before using. Generally served cold with salads, but delicious hot with parsley sauce or melted butter.
Brussels sprouts Should be firm, tight and green, never slimy.
To prepare Mark a cross with a sharp knife at base of each sprout. Boil rapidly like cabbage.
Cabbage, spring, summer or Savoy Should be firm and green and feel heavy for its size, so indicating a good heart.
To prepare Shred finely with sharp knife and boil rapidly for about 10 minutes in salted water. Serve raw in salads.
Cauliflower The flower should be white and firm. If slightly brown it is either stale or has been affected by frost.
To prepare Cut off thick stalks and outer leaves, divide head into small springs, cook rapidly in boiling salted water for about 10–20 minutes. Serve with white, parsley or cheese sauce. Cook large *broccoli heads* and *sprouting broccoli* in the same way.
Celery and chicory See salads.
Celeriac Large ugly root rather like a turnip. Should be firm without any bruises.
To prepare Generally eaten raw and in salads, but very good cooked. Peel and divide into neat pieces and cook in boiling salted water for about 20 minutes. Serve celeriac with white, parsley or cheese sauce.
Corn on the cob Pull back the outer leaves and the corn should be pale yellow and not too large. If very dark and very big it is old and likely to be tough.
To prepare Wash corn cob, strip off outer green leaves and boil in salted water for about 20 minutes, until the corn feels soft. Serve with a little melted butter. Do not boil too quickly or for too long, otherwise the corn becomes tough.
Cucumber See salads.
Eggplant or aubergine Should be firm, purple/black in colour with no bruises.
To prepare Wash and remove any hard stalk. Bake in a casserole with a knob of margarine and little milk for 30 minutes. Can be stuffed or fried like potatoes.
Endive See salads.
Fennel Rather like a root of celery, firm and white.
To prepare Cook like other vegetables, in boiling salted water and serve with a white sauce. 2–3-inch (5–7-cm.) pieces of fennel take about 10 minutes, for a firm texture. Particularly good served with fish or sliced and served raw.
Leeks Green part should be bright in colour. White root, firm, never slimy.
To prepare Cut off roots and outer leaves, split down the middle so they can be thoroughly washed. Use in place of onions in soups and stews, or boil for 30 minutes in salted water. Serve with white or cheese sauce.
Lettuce See salads.
Mushrooms Should be firm and light in colour on the top surface. A wrinkled looking mushroom is generally stale.
To prepare Can be fried or grilled in butter (see page 14) or baked in a covered casserole for about 30 minutes. Mushrooms can also be stewed in milk; the liquid is then thickened with a little flour or cornflour.
Onions Should be firm and the skin bright coloured.
To prepare Peel, slice or chop. Put into soups and stews, fried (see page 59) with meat or savoury dishes. As a separate vegetable boil for a good hour in salted water and serve with white sauce.
Parsnips Should not be shrivelled. This indicates they are very stale.
To prepare Peel and put into soups and stews, but do not have too large a proportion of parsnips as their flavour is very strong and will dominate the dish. Very good baked around the meat.
Peas Pods should be pale green, when yellow they are either very stale or very old.
To prepare Shell and cook steadily in boiling water for 10–15 minutes. Add little mint and a teaspoon of sugar to improve the flavour. Serve with a little melted butter.
Peppers Firm and bright in colour.
To prepare De-seed, shred and serve in salads. Can be baked and stuffed (see page 78).
Potatoes The colour of the skin depends on the variety. When new, rub skin slightly – it should come away easily. If it does not they are stale. Look for potatoes that have no imperfections.
To prepare Peel old potatoes, scrape new potatoes before cooking or remove peel when cooked. Always put into boiling salted water and cook steadily until soft. Can also be fried (see page 58), roasted, baked in their jackets or steamed.
Salsify (oyster plant) Should be firm and white.
To prepare Wash or scrape well, then cook as for Jerusalem artichokes. Serve with a little melted butter and chopped parsley.
Spinach Firm and green. The leaves become slimy when the vegetable is stale.
To prepare Wash leaves in several waters. There is no

need to add water to spinach, just put into a strong pan with a little salt and boil rapidly until tender, about 15 minutes. Either rub through a sieve or turn on to a board and chop finely, then return to the pan with a little milk and butter and reheat.

Tomatoes See salads. Can also be grilled or fried.

Turnips and swedes Should be firm without imperfections.

To prepare Peel and put into soups and stews. When young they are delicious cooked in boiling salted water, then mashed.

Vegetable marrow (Courgettes are tiny marrows); they should be firm to the touch and feel heavy for their size.

To prepare Peel and remove seeds from marrow (leave peel and seeds for courgettes), cut into neat pieces and then either steam over boiling salted water, adding a little salt, or boil in salted water until tender. Large pieces of marrow take approximately 15 minutes, whole courgettes approximately the same time. Sliced courgettes take approximately 5–8 minutes. Serve with cheese or white sauce. Can be baked with a stuffing (see pages 48–50).

Sweet potatoes or yams Prepare and cook as ordinary potatoes. You can recognise these by their bright pink skin. The nicest way to serve them is to roast them.

CORRECT COOKING OF VEGETABLES

In order to retain both colour and vitamin content in vegetables it is important to cook them with care. Unless stated to the contrary, green vegetables should go into a small quantity of boiling salted water – about 1 inch (2½ cm.) only in the pan – and in the case of a large amount of vegetables, like cabbage, should be added steadily rather than all at once. By putting into the water in this way the liquid keeps boiling. Cover the pan with a lid. Try and serve the vegetables immediately they are cooked, for if kept hot, even for a short time, you lose some vitamins.

Root vegetables need more water since they take longer to cook. Use approximately 1 pint (generous ½ litre; 2½ cups) water to each 1–1½ lb. (½–¾ kg.) of prepared vegetables. It is considered better to put the vegetables into boiling water as a green vegetable. Root vegetables, however, should be cooked very steadily, particularly potatoes, for if potatoes are boiled too quickly they become over soft on the outside before they are cooked through to the middle.

To strain vegetables

Either tilt the lid so that the liquid can be poured out, and pour the liquid into a container, or stand a colander in a container so you can retain the vegetable water, and pour the vegetables and water into this. Delicate vegetables such as cauliflower which break easily should be spooned into the colander.

To mash vegetables

Boil the vegetables – potatoes, carrots, turnips and swede are all suitable. Strain, then either break into pieces with a fork or vegetable masher or rub through a sieve and return to the pan. Add 1–2 oz. (25–50 g.; 2–4 tablespoons) butter or margarine to each 1 lb. (½ kg.) vegetables.

For creamy potatoes Gradually beat in 2–3 tablespoons warm milk.

To pipe potatoes

Smooth mashed potatoes may be piped as a border around the food. Use butter or margarine but *do not* add much milk otherwise the potato mixture will be too soft to keep its shape.

TO FRY POTATOES

Potatoes are the most usual vegetable to fry in deep fat and if cooked correctly they will be crisp and delicious.

Cooking time: few minutes

Serves 4

IMPERIAL · METRIC
12 oz./300 g. peeled potatoes
1 lb./½ kg. fat or 1 pint/generous ½ litre oil*

AMERICAN
¾ lb. peeled potatoes
1 lb. shortening or 2½ cups oil*

*Enough to come approximately half way up the pan when heated. Never have the pan more than half full.

Cut the potatoes either in slices or chips. Dry thoroughly in a clean cloth or kitchen paper. Heat the fat or oil. Test for correct heat. A cube of bread should turn brown in 30 seconds with oil, or 1 minute with fat. Or test by dropping in one chip or slice, which should rise to the top of the hot fat or oil and begin to cook immediately. If the fat is not sufficiently hot, wait and test again. Half fill the frying basket with slices or chips. Lower carefully into the hot fat or oil; turn the heat down under the pan. Cook steadily until the slices or chips are tender but only lightly browned. Lift the basket out of the fat, hold over pan to drain. Tip chips or slices on to a dish. Repeat with the next batch of dried potatoes. When all the chips or slices have been adequately fried, reheat the fat, test again, put in the potatoes and fry for a few moments until crisp and golden brown. Drain on crumpled absorbent paper.

FRIED ONIONS

Cooking time: 5–7 minutes

Serves 4

IMPERIAL · METRIC
12 oz./300 g. onions
3 tablespoons milk
1 oz./25 g. seasoned flour
3–4 oz./75–100 g. fat for shallow frying,
 or use deep fat (page 32)

AMERICAN
¾ lb. onions
scant ¼ cup milk
¼ cup seasoned flour
about ½ cup shortening for shallow
 frying, or use deep shortening
 (page 32)

Peel the onions and cut into rings. Separate the rings and dip first into the milk and then into the seasoned flour (see page 32 for instructions on coating). Shake to remove the surplus flour. Fry in either shallow fat for approximately 7 minutes, or deep fat for a shorter time until tender and golden brown. Drain the onions on absorbent paper before serving.

SALADS THAT MAKE A MEAL

Cheese All kinds make a meal with salad; grate, slice or dice the cheese and arrange with the vegetables. Remember cheese blends well with fruit, see page 61. Cottage cheese salad is excellent as a low calorie meal.
Eggs Both scrambled or hard-boiled are excellent with all salads.
Fish Shellfish, canned fish, white fish or herrings can be served with a green salad, mayonnaise or an oil and vinegar dressing.

Meats These can be given a new flavour by combining fruit with the more familiar salad ingredients. Try apple and/or prunes with pork, duck or veal; pineapple or peaches with ham; oranges or grapefruit with beef, duck or pork.

Some vegetable salads
Coleslaw This is made by shredding the heart of cabbage (preferably a white Dutch cabbage) and blending with mayonnaise. Other ingredients may be

Cottage cheese and pineapple salad

Scones (see page 75)

added such as grated carrot, chopped apple, chopped nuts, raisins and chopped celery. (*Illustrated on page* 49).

Potato salad This is made by dicing cooked potatoes (old or new) and blending with oil and vinegar or mayonnaise. Flavour with chopped chives, spring onions or a little grated onion and chopped parsley.

Russian salad Blend cooked, diced mixed vegetables such as carrots, turnips and beans with peas and mayonnaise.

Apple and nut salad (*Illustrated on page 52*). Mix chopped red-skinned apple with chopped celery and walnuts. Toss in mayonnaise or oil and vinegar dressing. Garnish with grapes and apple slices tossed in lemon juice.

EGG AND POTATO SALAD	IMPERIAL · METRIC	AMERICAN
	4 hard-boiled eggs	4 hard-cooked eggs
	12 oz./300 g. cooked potatoes	$\frac{3}{4}$ lb. cooked potatoes
Serves 4–6	1 dessert apple	1 dessert apple
	2 oz./50 g. carrot, grated	$\frac{2}{3}$ cup grated carrot
	6 spring onions	6 scallions
	4 tablespoons mayonnaise or oil and vinegar dressing (page 54)	$\frac{1}{3}$ cup mayonnaise or oil and vinegar dressing (page 54)
	chopped parsley	chopped parsley

Roughly chop the hard-boiled eggs. Mix the sliced potatoes, diced, cored apple (the peel may be kept on this), grated carrot and chopped spring onions, together with the mayonnaise or oil and vinegar dressing. Finally fold in the chopped egg. Place in a serving dish, sprinkle the top with chopped parsley. Serve with cold meat and poultry.

Cheese and potato salad
Follow the recipe above, but use 2 hard-boiled eggs and 6 oz. (150 g.; 1 cup) diced Cheddar cheese.

COTTAGE CHEESE AND PINEAPPLE SALAD	IMPERIAL · METRIC	AMERICAN
	1–2 heads chicory	1–2 heads endive
	1 bunch watercress	1 bunch watercress
Serves 2	2 tablespoons French dressing (page 54)	3 tablespoons French dressing (page 54)
	1 small can pineapple rings	1 small can pineapple rings
	8 oz./200 g. cottage cheese	1 cup cottage cheese
	2 tomatoes	2 tomatoes

Prepare the chicory and watercress (see pages 54 and 56), put on a plate and sprinkle with French dressing. Drain the pineapple rings. Place the cottage cheese in the centre of a salad platter and arrange the other ingredients around it.

Making batters

A batter is a mixture of flour, egg and liquid and is used for pancakes and Yorkshire puddings. It is essential to produce a smooth mixture and most people find plain flour (unless stated to the contrary) produces a better mixture. If you use 2–3 tablespoons water, rather than the full quantity of milk, a lighter batter will result.

BASIC PANCAKE BATTER	IMPERIAL · METRIC	AMERICAN
	4 oz./100 g. flour	1 cup all-purpose flour
	pinch salt	pinch salt
	1 egg	1 egg
Serves 4	$\frac{1}{2}$ pint/250 ml. milk or milk and water (see above)	$1\frac{1}{4}$ cups milk or milk and water (see above)

Put the flour and salt through a sieve into a bowl, add the egg and about a quarter of the liquid. Beat well with a wooden spoon to give a sticky consistency, then beat again until smooth. Gradually beat in the rest of the liquid. Allow to stand for a while in a cool place if time permits.

Pouring batter into the pan

Folding the finished pancake

TO MAKE PANCAKES

Cooking time: few minutes
each pancake

Serves 4*

IMPERIAL · METRIC
pancake batter (page 61)
filling
4 oz./100 g. cooking fat or lard, or
    4 tablespoons oil

AMERICAN
pancake batter (page 61)
filling
½ cup shortening or lard, or ⅓ cup oil

*This gives about eight 7-inch (18-cm.) pancakes.

Make the batter and transfer the mixture to a jug for easy pouring. Put about ½ oz. (15 g.; 1 tablespoon) fat or dessertspoon oil into the pan, heat steadily until melted and hot – there should be a *very faint* haze in pan. Pour just enough batter into pan to give a very thin coating. Cook steadily – lowering heat once the batter is set, for about 2 minutes; you can tell if pancake is cooked by shaking firmly – if it moves easily in pan, it is ready to turn or toss and cook on second side.

To turn, insert a broad-bladed knife or a fish slice under the centre of the pancake and carefully lift, then turn over, so the cooked side is uppermost.

To toss, hold the frying pan loosely in your hand with a *relaxed wrist*. Flick sharply upwards and with practice the pancake lifts in the air, turns over and drops back in pan with the cooked side uppermost.

Repeat with rest of the batter, adding fat before each pancake is cooked. As each pancake is cooked, lift on to sugared paper for sweet pancakes, then roll. If adding filling, put on to hot dish and keep hot, see opposite. When all the pancakes are cooked put in hot filling, roll and serve at once.

To keep pancakes hot
Put on to a really hot plate or dish. Stand the plate over a pan of boiling water, or put the uncovered dish into a cool oven.

Ways to serve and fill pancakes
Sweet
1 Put the cooked pancakes on to sugared paper. Roll and serve with sliced lemons or oranges.
2 Fill the pancakes with hot jam or a thick fruit purée.
3 Fill the pancakes with ice cream.

Savoury
1 Fill with a thick cheese sauce.
2 Fill with cooked spinach or cooked tomatoes.
3 Fill with Bolognese sauce (see page 53), made a little thicker than the recipe.

New look to pancakes
1 Do this by using the selection of fillings, above. You can use your imagination to provide interesting hot or cold fillings.
2 Sieve a good pinch of spice or ginger with the flour when making pancake batter.

Fritters

These are pieces of food, often fruit, coated with batter and fried until crisp and golden brown.

FRITTER BATTER

Cooking time: 4–5 minutes

IMPERIAL · METRIC
fritter batter
filling
3 oz./75 g. fat, or 3 tablespoons oil

AMERICAN
fritter batter
filling
scant ½ cup shortening, or scant ¼ cup oil

Serves 4

Recipe as pancake batter but use self-raising flour, or plain flour sieved with 1 teaspoon baking powder. Use only ¼ pint (125 ml.; ⅔ cup) liquid for thick coating (A); ⅓ pint (200 ml.; generous ¾ cup) liquid for thinner coating (B).
To cook fritters, make the batter (see page 61) and use to coat the filling. Heat the fat in a pan. Put in fritters, fry quickly on either side until crisp and brown, then reduce heat and cook steadily for about 6 minutes to make sure mixture is cooked through to the centre. Drain on absorbent paper.

Sweet and savoury fritters

Apples Peel and core cooking apples, cut into slices about ⅓ inch (1 cm.) thick. Dip in a little flour then thick coating batter A.
Bananas Cut across peeled banana, use either batter A or B.
Cauliflower Divide a cauliflower into neat pieces. Cook for about 5 minutes only in boiling salted water. Drain, coat in batter A. Fry and serve with grated cheese.
Cheese Coat triangular portions of processed cheese in batter B. Fry for about 2 minutes on each side.

MAKING AN OMELETTE

Cooking time: few minutes

IMPERIAL · METRIC
½–1 oz./15–25 g. butter
2 eggs
1–2 teaspoons water
seasoning
filling (optional, see below)

AMERICAN
1–2 tablespoons butter
2 eggs
1–2 teaspoons water
seasoning
filling (optional, see below)

Serves 1

Put the butter into a small omelette pan, approximately 5–6 inches (13–15 cm.) in diameter and heat gently. Meanwhile beat the eggs lightly with the water and seasoning; prepare the filling.
   Pour the eggs into the hot butter, wait a few seconds for a thin film to set at the bottom of the pan, then tilt the pan so the liquid egg runs to the side; meanwhile move the omelette away from the edge of the pan. Put in the filling, fold or roll away from the handle, tip on to a hot plate and serve at once.

Fillings for omelettes

1 Grated cheese or cream cheese. Put on top of the omelette before folding.
2 Sliced raw or cooked tomatoes.
3 Crisply fried bacon.
4 Diced cooked ham – blend with the eggs before cooking the omelette.

YORKSHIRE PUDDING

Cooking time: see method
Oven temperature:
450–475°F., 230–240°C.,
Gas Mark 8–9

IMPERIAL · METRIC
pancake batter (page 61)
1 oz./25 g. fat

AMERICAN
pancake batter (page 61)
2 tablespoons shortening

Serves 4

Make the batter. It can stand in a cool place if wished; but if the batter has been standing whisk sharply before cooking.
   For small puddings divide the fat between six to eight *deep* patty tins and heat for 3–5 minutes in a hot to very hot oven. Spoon the mixture in and bake for approximately 15 minutes towards top of a very hot oven. Reduce heat after 5–10 minutes if necessary.
   For a large pudding heat the fat as above allowing 5 minutes. Pour in the batter. Bake for approximately 30–40 minutes, reducing heat after 10–15 minutes.

Making pastry

There are many kinds of pastry, but the simplest is the short crust pastry (see below). The most important points to remember when making pastry are:
1 Weigh or measure accurately, so the basic proportions are not changed.
2 Keep everything as cool as possible.
3 Do not handle the pastry more than necessary.
4 Try not to make the pastry either too dry as it then becomes difficult to roll, or too wet as it then becomes sticky to handle and tough when cooked.

Amounts of pastry in recipes
When a recipe says 5 oz. (125 g.) pastry it does not mean 5 oz. (125 g.) pastry in weight – it means pastry made with 5 oz. (125 g.; 1¼ cups) flour etc.

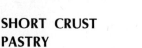

SHORT CRUST PASTRY

Cooking time: as recipe
Oven temperature: as recipe

IMPERIAL · METRIC
8 oz./200 g. flour
pinch salt
4 oz./100 g. fat*
2 tablespoons water

AMERICAN
2 cups all-purpose flour
pinch salt
½ cup fat*
about 3 tablespoons water

*All margarine, all lard or cooking fat (use a little less than 4 oz. (100 g.; ½ cup) of this), all butter, or 2 oz. (50 g.; ¼ cup) lard and 2 oz. (50 g.; ¼ cup) margarine.

Sieve the flour and salt into a mixing bowl, rub in the fat. Add the water gradually, using a palette knife. You need approximately 2 tablespoons water to bind 8 oz. flour and 4 oz. fat – slightly less if using the metric measures. The mixture is the correct consistency when it can be gathered into a ball, leaving the bowl quite clean. Do not use hard pressure. Put the pastry on to a lightly floured board, roll out to the required shape with a lightly floured rolling pin.

For sweet short crust pastry add 1 tablespoon sugar to the flour and salt before adding the fat.

SUET CRUST PASTRY

Cooking time: as recipe
Oven temperature: as recipe

IMPERIAL · METRIC
8 oz./200 g. flour
pinch salt
4 oz./100 g. suet
cold water to mix

AMERICAN
2 cups all-purpose flour
pinch salt
scant 1 cup finely chopped suet
cold water to mix

You can use plain flour without raising agent, but most people prefer a suet crust to rise slightly and either use self-raising flour or add 2 teaspoons baking powder to 8 oz. (200 g.; 2 cups) plain flour. If suet is bought from the butcher, remove the skin and chop or grate finely. Butchers' suet is easier to chop if a small amount of flour is shaken on to the chopping board. Most people prefer to buy shredded suet; this has been mixed with a very small amount of flour which helps it to keep for a long period.

Sieve the flour and salt into a mixing bowl. Add the suet and mix into the flour with a knife. Gradually stir the water into this mixture until it is soft enough to form into a ball but firm enough to roll out. Shake a little flour on the pastry board, put the ball of dough on this. Do not use too much flour, or the original proportion of fat to flour will be altered. Shake a very little flour over the rolling pin, roll the pastry out lightly and firmly. Suet crust pastry stretches a little more than short crust, but if handled carefully it keeps a good shape during cooking.

Puddings and desserts

There are many different kinds of puddings and desserts. In this section are baked and steamed puddings, fruit pies or flans as well as quick cold desserts.

BAKED FRUIT DUMPLINGS

Cooking time: see method
Oven temperature:
425–450°F., 220–230°C.,
Gas Mark 7–8, then
350–375°F., 180–190°C.,
Gas Mark 4–5

IMPERIAL · METRIC
12 oz.–1 lb./300–450 g. short crust pastry
(page 64)
4 apples or peaches, or 8 plums
sugar to taste
Glaze
1 egg white
Decoration
1 oz./25 g. castor sugar
1 tablespoon jam (optional)

AMERICAN
short crust pastry made with 3 or
4 cups all-purpose flour (page 64)
4 apples or peaches, or 8 plums
sugar to taste
Glaze
1 egg white
Decoration
2 tablespoons granulated sugar
1 tablespoon jam (optional)

Serves 4

The amount of pastry will depend upon the fruit to be coated. Large apples can take up to 4 oz. (100 g.) pastry. Smaller apples or large peaches will need only about 3 oz. (75 g.) pastry. If a large square is used and folded like an envelope you need rather more.

Make the pastry, roll out and cut into four or eight pieces. Prepare the fruit, peeling and coring apples. Put the fruit on to the pastry, sprinkle with the sugar, or fill the centres with the sugar. Wrap the pastry around the fruit, moisten the edges with water to seal thoroughly. Mould around the fruit. Put on to a baking tray. For shiny pastry, brush with egg white, but this is not necessary. Bake dumplings for approximately 15–20 minutes in the centre of a hot oven, then lower the heat to moderate to moderately hot for a further 35–40 minutes if cooking large apples, 25–30 minutes with medium apples or peaches. Sprinkle with sugar before serving and top with a little jam if wished. The dumplings may then be replaced in the oven so that the jam becomes hot.

TO MAKE A FLAN CASE AND FRUIT FLAN

Cooking time: 20–25 minutes
Oven temperature:
425–450°F., 220–230°C.,
Gas Mark 7–8

IMPERIAL · METRIC
5–6 oz./125–150 g. short crust or sweet
short crust pastry (opposite)

1 large can fruit
1 teaspoon arrowroot or cornflour

AMERICAN
short crust or sweet short crust pastry
using 2 cups all-purpose flour etc.
(opposite)
1 large can fruit
1 teaspoon arrowroot flour or cornstarch

Serves 4–6

Make the pastry and roll out until it is large enough to line a flan ring or tin, approximately 7 inches (18 cm.) in diameter. If using a flan ring put this on an upturned baking tray (this makes it easier to remove). The way to make sure the round of pastry is sufficiently large to line the ring or tin is to allow the diameter plus 1½ inches (3½ cm.) all round. When the pastry is inserted into the flan ring or tin press down firmly, then either cut nearly round or roll the rolling pin over the top, so the small amount of excess pastry falls away. Put greased greaseproof paper or foil into the pastry greasy side down. Cover with crusts of bread or haricot beans. Bake for 15 minutes in the centre of a hot oven. Remove the paper and lift away the flan ring. Cook for a further 5–10 minutes, until golden brown. This is known as baking blind.

To fill the flan case; drain the fruit well, arrange in the cold flan. Measure ¼ pint (125 ml.; ⅔ cup) of the juice. Blend with the arrowroot or cornflour, put into a saucepan and stir over a low heat until thickened and clear. Cool slightly, but do not allow to set, then either spread over the fruit with a flat-bladed knife or brush with a pastry brush.

BLACKCURRANT SAUCER PIES

Cooking time: 30 minutes
Oven temperature:
375–400°F., 190–200°C.,
Gas Mark 5–6

Serves 4

IMPERIAL · METRIC
10 oz./250 g. short crust or sweet short
    crust pastry (page 64)

12 oz./300 g. blackcurrants
2 oz./50 g. castor sugar
3 teaspoons cornflour or semolina

Decoration
little sugar
¼ pint/125 ml. double cream

AMERICAN
short crust or sweet short crust pastry
    using 2½ cups all-purpose flour etc.
    (page 64)
¾ lb. black currants
¼ cup granulated sugar
3 teaspoons cornstarch or semolina
    flour

Decoration
little sugar
⅔ cup whipping cream

Roll out the pastry and cut into eight circles large enough to line a saucer. Place a pastry circle on each saucer (use old saucers for baking). Mix the blackcurrants with the sugar. Sprinkle cornflour or semolina over the bottom of the pastry to absorb the surplus juice. Divide the fruit into four and place in the centre of each saucer. Moisten the edges of pastry, then put the second circle on top. Gently press the edges of the pastry together to seal, then trim the edges. Decorate with a fork or pointed knife. Bake in the centre of a moderately hot oven for 30 minutes. Sprinkle with castor sugar and serve hot or cold with whipped cream.

BISCUIT CRUMB FLAN

This is an excellent mixture
to use for a flan ring instead
of making pastry.

Cooking time: 12–15 minutes
Oven temperature:
350–375°F., 180–190°C.,
Gas Mark 4–5

Makes one 6–7 inch
(15–18-cm.) flan case

IMPERIAL · METRIC
2 oz./50 g. butter
2 oz./50 g. castor sugar
½ tablespoon golden syrup
4 oz./100 g. semi-sweet biscuits

AMERICAN
¼ cup butter
4 tablespoons sugar
½ tablespoon light corn syrup
¼ lb. semi-sweet cookies

Cream the butter, castor sugar and golden syrup together. Crush the biscuits into fine crumbs; to do this put the crumbs on one piece of greaseproof paper, cover with a second piece and roll firmly but carefully, so no crumbs are lost. Add to the creamed mixture. Press into a greased flan tin or ring. If wished, the mixture may be browned in a moderate to moderately hot oven, but this is not essential. Fill with fruit as given for a fruit flan on page 65.

EGG CUSTARD

Cooking time: see method
Oven temperature: 300°F.,
150°C., Gas Mark 2

Serves 2

IMPERIAL · METRIC
1 large egg
½ oz./15 g. sugar
½ pint/250 ml. milk
pinch grated nutmeg (optional)

AMERICAN
1 large egg
1 tablespoon sugar
1¼ cups milk
pinch grated nutmeg (optional)

To bake the custard: break the egg into a basin, add the sugar and beat for 1 minute. Pour on the milk. Strain the mixture into a 1-pint (½-litre) pie dish. This makes certain you have no particles of egg that have not blended with the milk. Top with a little grated nutmeg if desired. Stand the pie dish in another dish or tin containing cold water (called a bain-marie). Bake in the centre of a cool oven until firm, about 45 minutes.
For a firmer custard Use 2 eggs or 2 egg yolks only (the white can be used for meringues).
To steam the custard Make as above and strain into the dish. Cover with greased paper or foil. Place in a steamer over a pan of hot, but not boiling, water.

Steam for approximately 40 minutes until firm. The water in the steamer *must not be allowed to boil.*

To boil* the custard Make as above and strain into the top of a double saucepan with hot, but not boiling, water underneath. Cook slowly, stirring from time to time with a wooden spoon until the mixture is sufficiently thick to coat the spoon. Serve as a sauce with fruit or other puddings.

*This is the name given to this method of cooking custard. But as you will see the custard *never boils,* it cooks gently. If you have no double saucepan, then use a basin which should fit securely over a saucepan of hot water.

ROSY APPLE CUSTARD

This is an excellent way of preparing a delicious dessert, based on custard.

Cooking time: 10 minutes

Serves 4

IMPERIAL · METRIC	AMERICAN
2½ tablespoons custard powder	3½ tablespoons cornstarch*
1 pint/generous ½ litre milk	2½ cups milk*
2 tablespoons rose hip syrup	3 tablespoons rose hip syrup
4 rosy dessert apples	4 rosy dessert apples
3 teaspoons lemon juice	3 teaspoons lemon juice

*If liked 2½ cups custard (see page 66) may be used in place of the cornstarch and milk.

Make the custard with powder and milk following instructions on the packet. When thickened remove from the heat, cool slightly and add the rose hip syrup. Wash the apples, dry and grate three of them coarsely – the peel need not be removed. Blend with the rose hip flavoured custard. Put into four dishes or sundae glasses. Allow to cool. Meanwhile cut the remaining apple into thin slices, remove the core, but retain the peel. Dip into lemon juice to preserve colour and arrange on top of the dessert.

Note Sugar is not included in the ingredients but add a little to the custard if desired.

LEMON MERINGUE PIE

Illustrated on the jacket

Cooking time: 1 hour
Oven temperature:
425–450°F., 220–230°C.,
Gas Mark 7–8 then
275–300°F., 140–145°C.,
Gas Mark 1–2, or 225–250°F.,
110–130°C., Gas Mark ¼–½

IMPERIAL · METRIC	AMERICAN
6 oz./170 g. short crust or sweet short crust pastry (page 64)	short crust or sweet short crust pastry using 1½ cups all-purpose flour etc. (page 64)
4 tablespoons cornflour	⅓ cup cornstarch
½ pint/250 ml. water	1¼ cups water
1 oz./25 g. butter	2 tablespoons butter
grated rind and juice of 2 lemons	grated rind and juice of 2 lemons
8 oz./200 g. castor sugar	1 cup granulated sugar
2 eggs	2 eggs

Serves 4–6

Make the pastry and roll out to line a deep 7–8-inch (18–20-cm.) flan ring on an upturned baking sheet or tray (see page 65), or a deep pie plate or ovenproof flan dish. Bake blind in a hot oven until just golden brown; this takes approximately 20 minutes. Meanwhile, blend the cornflour to a smooth paste with a little of the cold water.

Bring the butter and the rest of the water to the boil, pour over the blended cornflour, stirring well. Put into a saucepan and cook for 3–5 minutes, stirring all the time, as the mixture becomes very thick. Remove from the heat, stir in the lemon rind and juice and half the sugar. Separate the yolks from the whites of the eggs. Stir the egg yolks into the cool lemon mixture; pour into the flan case. Whisk the egg whites until stiff, gradually beat in 2 oz. (50 g.; ¼ cup) castor sugar, then fold in the remaining 2 oz. (50 g.; ¼ cup) sugar. Pile on top of the lemon mixture; make sure that the meringue touches the edge of the pastry all round, to prevent it forming a moist layer when cooked. Place in the centre of a cool oven for 25–30 minutes, or until the meringue is firm and only lightly browned. If serving cold, bake the pie for approximately 1–1¼ hours in a very cool oven to make sure meringue remains crisp.

Note If serving hot, 2 oz. (50 g.; ¼ cup) sugar only could be used with the 2 egg whites. If liked, the meringue may be piped over the lemon filling.

BASIC SWEET SOUFFLE

Cooking time: 25–30 minutes
Oven temperature:
375–400°F., 190–200°C.,
Gas Mark 5–6

Serves 4

IMPERIAL · METRIC	AMERICAN
1 tablespoon cornflour	1 tablespoon cornstarch
$\frac{1}{4}$ pint/125 ml. milk	$\frac{2}{3}$ cup milk
3–4 eggs	3–4 eggs
$\frac{1}{2}$–1 oz./15–25 g. butter or margarine	1–2 tablespoons butter or margarine
2 oz./50 g. sugar	4 tablespoons sugar
flavouring (see below)	flavoring (see below)
1 tablespoon icing sugar	1 tablespoon confectioners' sugar

Blend the cornflour with the milk until smooth; put into a saucepan and bring the mixture to the boil over a moderate heat, stirring all the time until thick. Separate the egg yolks from the egg whites. Remove the saucepan containing the sauce from the heat and stir in the butter or margarine and sugar, then gradually beat in the egg yolks with a wooden spoon. Add the flavouring. Whisk the egg whites until stiff and fold into the sauce and egg yolk mixture with a metal spoon. Put into a soufflé dish, place on a baking sheet and bake in centre of a moderately hot oven for 25–30 minutes, until well risen and firm. Dust the top of the soufflé with a tablespoon of sieved icing sugar. (Make sure the icing sugar is all ready before the soufflé is brought from the oven.)

Flavourings for a sweet soufflé
Do not exceed the amount of flavouring, otherwise the mixture becomes too heavy and will not rise properly.

Chocolate Either blend 1 oz. (25 g.; $\frac{1}{4}$ cup) sieved cocoa powder, or use 2 oz. (50 g.; $\frac{1}{2}$ cup) chocolate powder, with the sauce. As chocolate powder is sweetened, a little less sugar may be used. A better flavour is given if $\frac{1}{4}$ teaspoon vanilla essence is also added.
Coffee Either blend 2 teaspoons instant coffee powder with the milk, or add 1 tablespoon coffee essence to the milk or use $\frac{1}{4}$ pint (125 ml.; $\frac{2}{3}$ cup) strong black coffee in place of milk.
Pineapple Open a small can of pineapple, drain the syrup from the fruit, use $\frac{1}{4}$ pint (125 ml.; $\frac{2}{3}$ cup) of this in place of the milk. Chop the canned fruit finely and add to the sauce when thickened. Because this filling is rather sweet, 1 oz. (25 g.; 2 tablespoons) sugar only need be used.
Lemon or orange Add the grated rind of 1–2 lemons or oranges to the cornflour, squeeze the juice from the fruit and if necessary add enough water to give $\frac{1}{4}$ pint (125 ml.; $\frac{2}{3}$ cup). Use in place of the milk.

GOLDEN APRICOT PUDDING

Cooking time: 1 hour–
1 hour 10 minutes
Oven temperature:
325–350°F., 170–180°C.,
Gas Mark 3–4

Serves 5–6

IMPERIAL · METRIC	AMERICAN
1 lb./$\frac{1}{2}$ kg. fresh apricots	1 lb. fresh apricots
$\frac{1}{4}$ pint/125 ml. water	$\frac{2}{3}$ cup water
4 oz./100 g. soft brown sugar	$\frac{1}{2}$ cup brown sugar
Topping	**Topping**
3 oz./75 g. butter	scant $\frac{1}{2}$ cup butter
3 oz./75 g. sugar	6 tablespoons sugar
4 oz./100 g. self-raising flour	1 cup all-purpose flour sifted with 1 teaspoon baking powder
4 tablespoons milk	$\frac{1}{3}$ cup milk
3 egg whites	3 egg whites
1 oz./25 g. almonds	about $\frac{1}{4}$ cup whole almonds
Golden sauce	**Golden sauce**
3 egg yolks	3 egg yolks
1 oz./25 g. castor sugar	2 tablespoons granulated sugar
3 tablespoons apricot juice	scant $\frac{1}{4}$ cup apricot juice
1 teaspoon lemon juice	1 teaspoon lemon juice

Halve and stone the apricots. Heat the water with the sugar in a large saucepan until the sugar has dissolved, then add the halved apricots to the hot syrup and simmer gently for 5 minutes, until they are just becoming soft. Strain the fruit carefully and save the juice. Put the fruit into a well-buttered 8-inch (20-cm.) round ovenproof dish.

To prepare the topping; cream the butter and sugar until soft and light (see page 11). Sift the flour and fold into the butter mixture with the milk. Whisk the egg whites until very stiff and fold into the topping mixture; spread this over the apricots. Blanch and flake the almonds (see opposite). Sprinkle over the top of the sponge mixture and bake for 50 minutes to 1 hour in the centre of a moderate oven until firm to the touch.

To make the sauce; whisk the egg yolks and sugar together in a basin until frothy, then slowly whisk in the apricot juice and lemon juice etc., 10 minutes before serving the pudding. Put over a pan of hot *not* boiling water and whisk until thickened. This sauce is delicious but must be made at the last minute and served hot as soon as it is made. If preferred serve the pudding with fresh cream (the egg yolks can be used for other dishes, see page 66).

Golden apricot pudding

Festival Alaska

FESTIVAL ALASKA

Cooking time: 3–5 minutes
Oven temperature:
475–500°F., 240–250°C.,
Gas Mark 9–10

Serves 6–8

IMPERIAL · METRIC
8–9-inch (20–23-cm.) baked flan case
  (page 65)
about 12 oz./300 g. mincemeat
3 egg whites
3 oz./75 g. castor sugar
1 large block vanilla ice cream

AMERICAN
8–9-inch baked flan case (page 65)

about 1 cup mincemeat
3 egg whites
6 tablespoons granulated sugar
1 large block vanilla ice cream

Fill the flan case with the mincemeat. Whisk the egg whites until very stiff, gradually whisk in half the sugar, fold in the rest of the sugar. Cut the ice cream into six even portions and pile on top of the mincemeat. Spoon or pipe the meringue over the ice cream to completely enclose it and flash in the very hot *preheated* oven for about 3–5 minutes, until the top is a pale golden brown.

Serve immediately if possible.

Other Alaskas
All kinds of fruit may be used in an Alaska.
Note While this dessert is better eaten immediately the meringue is browned, it can keep for about 20 minutes after baking.

AUSTRIAN APPLE TORTE

Cooking time: 30 minutes
Oven temperature: 375°F.,
190°C., Gas Mark 5

Serves 6–8

IMPERIAL · METRIC
10 oz./250 g. sweet short crust pastry
  (page 64)
1½ lb./¾ kg. dessert apples
juice of 1 lemon
grated rind of ½ lemon
2 tablespoons sugar
4 oz./100 g. blanched flaked almonds
  (see below)
Glaze
1 egg

AMERICAN
sweet short crust pastry made with
  2½ cups all-purpose flour (page 64)
1½ lb. dessert apples
juice of 1 lemon
grated rind of ½ lemon
3 tablespoons sugar
1 cup blanched flaked almonds (see
  below)
Glaze
1 egg

Roll out the pastry and use to line a 9-inch (23-cm.) flan ring on an upturned baking tray (see page 65). Reserve the pastry trimmings. Core and slice but do not peel the apples, arrange in the pastry case, sprinkling with lemon juice, rind and sugar. Scatter three-quarters of the almonds over the top. Roll out the pastry trimmings, cut in strips and use to form lattice pattern over the apple filling. Brush with beaten egg

and scatter with the remaining almonds. Bake the torte in centre of a moderately hot oven for about 30 minutes, reducing the heat after 20 minutes if necessary.
To blanch almonds
Put the almonds into boiling water for about 1 minute, strain and when cool enough to handle remove the skins. To flake almonds, split them with a sharp knife.

69

CHRISTMAS PUDDING

Cooking time: see method

Serves 6–8

IMPERIAL · METRIC	AMERICAN
2 oz./50 g. flour or cornflour	½ cup all-purpose flour or cornstarch
2 oz./50 g. breadcrumbs	1 cup fresh soft bread crumbs
½ teaspoon mixed spice	½ teaspoon mixed spice
1 teaspoon powdered cinnamon	1 teaspoon powdered cinnamon
1 teaspoon grated nutmeg	1 teaspoon grated nutmeg
2 tablespoons corn oil	3 tablespoons corn oil
2 oz./50 g. brown sugar	4 tablespoons brown sugar
2 oz./50 g. apple, grated	⅔ cup grated apple
1 small carrot, grated	1 small carrot, grated
2 oz./50 g. mixed candied peel, chopped	scant ½ cup chopped candied peel
4 tablespoons ale, beer, stout or milk	⅓ cup ale, beer, stout or milk
2 oz./50 g. currants	scant ½ cup currants
4 oz./100 g. raisins	scant 1 cup raisins
2 oz./50 g. sultanas	scant ½ cup seedless white raisins
1–2 oz./25–50 g. chopped blanched almonds (optional)	¼–½ cup chopped blanched almonds (optional)
grated rind and juice of ½ lemon	grated rind and juice of ½ lemon
grated rind of ½ orange	grated rind of ½ orange
½ tablespoon golden syrup or black treacle	½ tablespoon maple syrup or black treacle
2 eggs	2 eggs

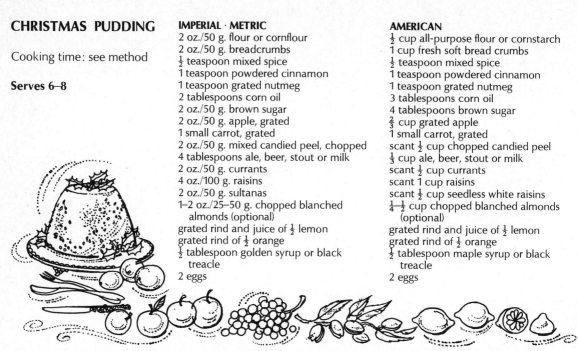

Make sure the bread is not too stale, for the pudding could become mouldy if very old bread is used. If the fruit has been washed (not often necessary with packet fruit) allow to dry for 48 hours before using.

Mix all the ingredients together and either put into one greased large basin or two smaller basins. Cover with greased greaseproof paper or foil. Steam the large pudding for at least 5 hours, the smaller ones for a minimum of 3 hours. Take off the damp covers and put on dry covers. Store in a cool dry place. Steam for a further 2 hours on Christmas day.

Fruit suet pudding

Make the suet crust pastry as on page 64 using 8 oz. (200 g.; 2 cups) flour, then roll out the pastry using about two-thirds of the dough. Line the basin. Fill with 1¼ lb. (¾ kg.) prepared fruit and sugar to taste. If using all apples add 2–3 tablespoons water to provide the juice, but blackberries are soft so no water is needed. if liked, a few sultanas can be mixed with the apples.

Top the pudding with the remainder of the suet crust pastry, and cover as steak and kidney pudding (see page 45). Steam for 2½ hours over boiling water. Turn out carefully and serve with hot custard sauce or cream.

To cook fruit

Fresh fruit Either put the prepared fruit with a little water and sugar to taste into the pan and simmer gently. Better still, make a syrup of sugar and water first, then add the fruit and cook gently. This method keeps the fruit more firm. To 1 lb. (½ kg.) fruit allow 2–3 oz. (50–75 g.; about ¼ cup) sugar and up to 4 table-spoons water with juicy fruit; the same amount of sugar but ¼ pint (125 ml.; ⅔ cup) water for fairly firm fruit; the same amount of sugar and ½ pint (250 ml.; 1¼ cups) water if the fruit is really hard (under-ripe gooseberries, for example).

Dried fruit Soak the fruit overnight in 1 pint (generous ½ litre; 2½ cups) water. Add sugar to taste and simmer for about 45 minutes–1 hour.

Fruit salad

The colour picture on page 56 shows an interesting mixture of fresh fruit – sliced apples and pears, seg-ments of fresh orange and grapefruit, banana slices, black and green grapes and glacé cherries. Make a syrup with 2 oz. (50 g.; ¼ cup) sugar and ¼ pint (125 ml.; ⅔ cup) orange juice.

Other fruit salads can be made by blending canned fruit and the syrup from the can with fresh fruit.

Fruit jelly

Fresh fruit may be put into a jelly. The only exception is fresh pineapple which prevents a jelly setting, but it can always be used as decoration. Remember that fresh fruit (except bananas) provides a certain amount of liquid so be sparing in the amount of liquid for set-ting the jelly – use about 1 tablespoon less when you are making a 1-pint (½-litre) jelly. Canned or cooked fruit is excellent in jellies. Drain the syrup or juice from the fruit, add sufficient water to give the quantity for setting the jelly. Always follow manufacturers' instruc-tions on packets.

HONEY COFFEE PUDDINGS

Cooking time: 30 minutes

Serves 6

IMPERIAL · METRIC	AMERICAN
4 oz./100 g. butter	½ cup butter
2 oz./50 g. soft brown sugar	4 tablespoons brown sugar
2 tablespoons thick honey	3 tablespoons thick honey
2 eggs	2 eggs
6 oz./150 g. self-raising flour	1½ cups all-purpose flour sifted with 1½ teaspoons baking powder
2 tablespoons coffee essence	3 tablespoons strong black coffee

Grease six ¼-pint (125-ml.; ⅔-cup) moulds, or use old teacups, then line the bottoms with circles of greased greaseproof paper. Cream the butter, sugar and honey together until light and fluffy. Beat in the eggs, gradually adding a little of the sieved flour with the last amount of egg. Add the coffee essence. Fold in the remaining sieved flour. Divide the mixture between the moulds or cups. Cover the tops with a double layer of greased foil and steam for 30 minutes. Serve with hot coffee sauce.

HOT COFFEE SAUCE

Serves 6

IMPERIAL · METRIC	AMERICAN
1 oz./25 g. cornflour	¼ cup cornstarch
1 pint/generous ½ litre milk	2½ cups milk
1½ oz./40 g. sugar	3 tablespoons sugar
3 tablespoons coffee essence	scant ¼ cup strong black coffee

Blend the cornflour with 2 tablespoons milk; bring the remaining milk to the boil, then pour over the blended cornflour. Return to the heat, add the sugar and bring to the boil, stirring until the sauce has thickened. Remove from the heat and stir in the coffee essence.

Cheese

Cheese is one of the most useful foods, it is therefore important to recognise good cheese, and to choose a wide selection of cheese to give variety. Never buy too large a quantity of one kind if you are a small family for it can become stale. See the recommendations about storing cheese on page 6. Only certain cheeses can be used in cooking and these are mentioned in the following lists.

Caerphilly A famous Welsh cheese, creamy white and mild. Not suitable for cooking.

Cheddar Close textured and creamy in colour. From Britain, Canada, Australia, New Zealand, France. Also red in colour. Eat uncooked or use in cooking.

Cheshire Either more golden than Cheddar, or white in colour, similar flavour. From Britain. Eat uncooked or use in cooking.

Cottage cheese Made in Britain. A crumbly low calorie cheese. Generally served in salads.

Derby Like Cheddar in appearance. From Britain. Not suitable for cooking.

Double Gloucester Very smooth texture, like Cheddar in flavour. From Britain. Not suitable for cooking.

Lancashire Stronger in flavour than Cheshire, white in colour. From Britain. Eat uncooked or use in cooking.

Leicester Deep gold colour, milk flavour. From Britain. Not suitable for cooking.

Stilton A blue-veined cheese, very strong flavour; a rather expensive luxury cheese. From Britain. Not suitable for cooking.

Camembert and Brie Two soft cheeses from France, although they are also available from Denmark, Ireland, Sweden and other countries. Not suitable for cooking. Must be soft to be palatable. If very firm, they are not ripe. Ripe is the term which is given to cheese at its best.

Cream cheese Comes from various countries, Switzerland being particularly famous. This is generally eaten uncooked, but it can be added to sauces.

Danish Blue Comes from Denmark. A blue-veined cheese, strong in flavour. Not suitable for use in cooking.

Edam (red skin) and Gouda (white skin) Two popular Dutch cheeses, mild in flavour. Use for cooking or eat uncooked.

Gorgonzola An Italian cheese similar to Danish blue in flavour. Not usually suitable for cooking.

Gruyère and Emmental Two Swiss cheeses. Can be eaten uncooked. Very fine, but expensive, cooking cheeses.

Parmesan A very hard Italian cheese. Can be bought in drums ready grated. Used only in cooking, too strong a flavour to eat uncooked.

CHEESE PUDDING

Cooking time: 35–40 minutes
Oven temperature:
350–375°F., 180–190°C.,
Gas Mark 4–5

Serves 3–4

IMPERIAL · METRIC	AMERICAN
½ pint/250 ml. milk	1¼ cups milk
½ oz./15 g. butter or margarine	1 tablespoon butter or margarine
pinch salt	pinch salt
pinch pepper	pinch pepper
2 oz./50 g. soft breadcrumbs	1 cup fresh soft bread crumbs
6 oz./150 g. Cheddar cheese, grated	1½ cups grated Cheddar cheese
1 egg	1 egg

Bring the milk to the boil, add the butter or margarine, the salt and pepper and pour over the breadcrumbs. Add the cheese and stir until melted. Beat the egg into the breadcrumb mixture. Pour into a well-greased pie dish and bake in the centre of a moderate to moderately hot oven for 35–40 minutes, until firm and brown.

CHEESE SCOTCH EGGS

Cooking time: 12 minutes

Serves 4

IMPERIAL · METRIC	AMERICAN
4 eggs	4 eggs
6 oz./150 g. Cheddar cheese, grated	1½ cups grated Cheddar cheese
1½ oz./40 g. flour	6 tablespoons all-purpose flour
½ teaspoon salt	½ teaspoon salt
pinch cayenne pepper	pinch cayenne pepper
½ teaspoon Worcestershire sauce	½ teaspoon Worcestershire sauce
1 egg	1 egg
1–2 tablespoons milk	1–3 tablespoons milk
Coating	**Coating**
1½ oz./40 g. crisp breadcrumbs	scant ½ cup fine dry bread crumbs
oil or fat for deep frying	oil or shortening for deep frying
Garnish	**Garnish**
parsley	parsley

Put the eggs into a pan of water, cook for 10 minutes then crack the shells (see page 13). Mix the grated cheese, flour and seasoning, add sauce, the beaten egg and milk and beat well.

Using wet hands coat the hard-boiled eggs completely with the cheese mixture. Roll them in crisp breadcrumbs. Fry in hot deep oil or fat for 2 minutes to allow the cheese mixture to cook through and to brown. Drain on absorbent paper, cool slightly and cut across in half. Serve, garnished with parsley and with a mixed salad (see page 54).

WELSH RAREBIT

This traditional recipe is sometimes called Welsh rabbit. There are many ways to make it but this recipe is a simple one which gives a good result.

Cooking time: few minutes

Serves 4

IMPERIAL · METRIC	AMERICAN
1 oz./25 g. butter	2 tablespoons butter
4 oz./100 g. Cheddar* cheese, grated	1 cup grated Cheddar* cheese
½ teaspoon made mustard	½ teaspoon made mustard
pinch salt	pinch salt
shake pepper	shake pepper
1 tablespoon milk or ale	1 tablespoon milk or ale
few drops Worcestershire sauce	few drops Worcestershire sauce
2 slices bread	2 slices bread
Garnish	**Garnish**
parsley or watercress	parsley or watercress

*It is usual for grated Cheddar cheese to be used, but Dutch or Lancashire can give a change of flavour. Larger quantities of Welsh rarebit may be prepared and stored in a screw-top jar in a cool place.

Put the butter into a basin, cream with a wooden spoon, then add the rest of ingredients except the bread. Toast the bread, remove crusts if wished, spread with the rarebit mixture. Heat the grill and cook the Welsh rarebit mixture until brown. Serve at once garnished with parsley or watercress.

When you entertain

Do not imagine the dishes you make when entertaining need to be very complicated. Use some of those dishes you know you cook well and serve them with extra garnishes or add an extra course to the meal.

Choosing wines

Your wine merchant will help you choose good wines and although a great deal is written about the right wine to serve with the right food it really is a matter of personal taste. However, a safe rule is to serve a white wine, which should be lightly chilled, with foods with a delicate flavour such as fish, white meat (veal) and chicken. Some well known white wines are: Graves: Pouilly-Fuissé, Chablis.

A red wine, should be opened about ½–1 hour before a meal, so it can be slightly warmed – it is described as being served at room temperature. Good red wines, which are generally available, are: Beaujolais, Mâcon, St. Emilion, Nuits St. Georges.

Suggestions for adding a more interesting touch to familiar food are given below.

Informal parties

A cheese and wine party, see below, would be an excellent choice, and a selection of dips served with small cheese biscuits, potato crisps and pieces of celery is much easier and quicker to prepare than cocktail savouries. Suggestions for these are below.

Planning a buffet party

For this party you could choose the following: melon cut in dice and served in glasses. Lamb pies (see page 42) and salad. Oranges in syrup, see below. Cinnamon and almond slices, see below. All these dishes could be prepared beforehand and cooked at the last minute.

ORANGES IN SYRUP

Cooking time: 15 minutes

Serves 12

IMPERIAL · METRIC	AMERICAN
12 medium-sized oranges	12 medium-sized oranges
1 pint/generous ½ litre water	2½ cups water
8 oz./200 g. sugar	1 cup sugar
2 tablespoons orange-flavoured liqueur (Curaçao)	3 tablespoons orange-flavored liqueur (Curaçao)

Cut the zest (top yellow part) thinly from six of the oranges. Peel the pith away from these and the other oranges. Cut oranges into ¼-inch (½-cm.) thick slices, take out any pips and place slices in serving dish. Put the orange zest, water and sugar in a pan. Allow the sugar to dissolve over a low heat, cover and simmer gently for about 15 minutes. Cool slightly then strain over the oranges and add the liqueur. Chill.
Note Make the day before the party and keep in a covered container.

CINNAMON AND ALMOND SLICES

Cooking time: 20 minutes
Oven temperature:
350–375°F., 180–190°C.,
Gas Mark 4–5

Makes 18

IMPERIAL · METRIC	AMERICAN
4 oz./100 g. butter	½ cup butter
2 oz./50 g. castor sugar	¼ cup sugar
6 oz./150 g. plain flour	1½ cups all-purpose flour
½ teaspoon powdered cinnamon	½ teaspoon powdered cinnamon
Glaze	**Glaze**
1 egg	1 egg
1 oz./25 g. blanched flaked almonds (page 69)	¼ cup blanched flaked almonds (page 69)
½ oz./15 g. granulated sugar	1 tablespoon granulated sugar

Cream the butter and sugar together until light and fluffy. Add the sieved flour with the cinnamon and work the mixture well together. Press into a buttered Swiss roll tin 7 inches (18 cm.) by 11 inches (28 cm.), then flatten with a knife. Brush with the beaten egg and prick with a fork. Sprinkle the almonds and granulated sugar over the top. Bake in centre of a moderate to moderately hot oven for 20 minutes, until golden brown. Mark into 18 fingers while still warm. These may be made one or two days before the party and kept in an airtight tin away from cakes or other biscuits.

CHEESE AND WINE PARTY

This type of party has become very popular, for the food is satisfying and the preparations simple.
Cheese Allow at least 3 oz. (75 g.) per head (have cream cheese, Cheddar, Cheshire, Camembert or Brie, Danish blue or Gorgonzola or Stilton, and any other varieties you wish). Arrange the cheeses on boards with a

garnish of radishes, lettuce, celery, tomatoes.

Biscuits Have a variety, including crispbread, and allow about 1 lb. (½ kg.) to every eight people.

Bread Choose crusty French bread. One long loaf serves about eight (with biscuits as well).

Butter You will need about 12 oz. (300 g.) for eight people and if space is limited, butter the thick slices of bread and the biscuits.

Extras Cheese blends with everything, so have:

Halved hard-boiled eggs topped with cream cheese.

Cubes of melon, canned pineapple, orange segments, on cocktail sticks.

Olives, gherkins, pickled onions, wedges of fresh tomato, lots of radishes and crisp lettuce.

Other fresh fruit such as apples, grapes, pears.

Drinks Red or white wines blend with cheese and so will a well-chilled vin rosé but the men may prefer beer or lager. See page 73 for information on wine.

DEVILLED EGG DIP

Cooking time: few minutes

Serves 4–5

IMPERIAL · METRIC	AMERICAN
4 hard-boiled eggs	4 hard-cooked eggs
1 carton natural yoghourt	1 carton unflavored yogurt
1 oz./25 g. butter	2 tablespoons butter
1 onion	1 onion
2 teaspoons curry powder	2 teaspoons curry powder
½ teaspoon tomato ketchup or chilli sauce	½ teaspoon tomato catsup or chili sauce
seasoning	seasoning
very little desiccated coconut (optional)	very little shredded coconut (optional)

Shell and chop the eggs very finely then blend with the yoghourt and allow to stand for a while.

Meanwhile, heat the butter, fry the peeled and grated onion in this until soft, then add the curry

powder and ketchup and blend with the eggs and seasoning. Top with the coconut if wished. This is excellent with sprigs of raw cauliflower as dippers.

PINEAPPLE CHEESE DIP

Serves 4–5

IMPERIAL · METRIC	AMERICAN
1 small can pineapple pieces	1 small can pineapple pieces
2 oz./50 g. walnuts	½ cup walnuts
¼ pint/125 ml. double cream	⅔ cup whipping cream
6 oz./150 g. Cheshire cheese, finely grated	1½ cups finely grated Cheshire or Cheddar cheese
seasoning	seasoning

Drain and chop the pineapple and nuts, whip the cream until it holds its shape, then add the cheese

and seasoning. Blend with the pineapple and nuts. Serve with halved walnuts, sticks of celery and crisps.

QUICK TIPS FOR PARTY FARE

Hors d'oeuvre

Top halved grapefruit with a little butter, honey and cinnamon. Heat under the grill.

Blend equal quantities of lightly whipped cream, mayonnaise and tomato purée to form a delicious sauce for shellfish cocktails or salads. Season well and add a little finely grated lemon rind and juice to taste.

Meat

Add a carton of yoghourt, a little finely chopped onion or chives and a few capers to the butter remaining in the pan after frying pork or veal. Heat for 1 minute, pour over the meat.

Add a good knob of butter to apple sauce to serve with pork, for a richer flavour.

Desserts

Blend 2 peeled grated dessert apples, some chopped

dates and chopped nuts with a block of dairy ice cream. Pile in glasses and top with cream and nuts.

Remove the peel from 3 large oranges and cut into rings. Stir 2 oz. (50 g.; ¼ cup) butter and 3 oz. (75 g.; 6 tablespoons) sugar together until golden coloured in a large frying pan. Add the orange slices and turn in the butterscotch mixture. Serve with cream.

Quick savouries

Split tiny cocktail sausages, insert piece Cheddar cheese. Roll in bacon, secure with wooden cocktail sticks and grill or bake.

Halve hard-boiled eggs and blend the yolks with:

1 Cream cheese and chutney.
2 Chopped ham and horseradish cream.
3 Chopped prawns and mayonnaise.
4 Little butter and chopped fresh herbs.

Pile filling into egg white cases and serve on lettuce.

Tea time

Of the many dishes suitable for tea time, I have selected just a few that are very simple to make, biscuits, scones and an uncooked cake.

A leisurely tea time is one of the pleasures of weekends for most people, so make sure you can produce an interesting tea table when required.

SCONES

Illustrated on page 60

Cooking time: 10 minutes
Oven temperature:
450–475°F., 230–240°C.,
Gas Mark 8–9

Makes 10–12 small scones

IMPERIAL · METRIC
8 oz./200 g. self-raising flour,* or use plain flour with either 4 teaspoons baking powder, or 1 teaspoon cream of tartar and ½ teaspoon bicarbonate of soda
good pinch salt
1–2 oz./25–50 g. butter or margarine
1 oz./25 g. sugar
milk to mix

AMERICAN
2 cups all-purpose flour with 4 teaspoons baking powder, or 1 teaspoon cream of tartar and ½ teaspoon baking soda

good pinch salt
2–4 tablespoons butter or margarine
2 tablespoons sugar
milk to mix

*If self-raising flour is used 2 teaspoons baking powder can be added, if liked.

Sieve together the flour, bicarbonate of soda and cream of tartar if used, and salt into a bowl. Rub in butter or margarine. Add the sugar. Mix to a soft rolling consistency with the milk. Roll out and cut into the required shapes. Put on to an ungreased baking sheet. Brush the tops with milk or beaten egg, if liked and

bake near the top of a very hot oven for approximately 10 minutes. To test if cooked, press firmly at the sides. Scones are cooked when they feel firm to the touch. Cool on a wire tray, then split and spread with butter, or serve with jam and cream.

CHOCOLATE REFRIGERATOR CAKE

Makes 9–12 slices

IMPERIAL · METRIC
12 oz./300 g. plain chocolate
4 oz./100 g. luxury margarine*
4 oz./100 g. castor sugar
5 oz./125 g. digestive biscuits, crushed
1 teaspoon vanilla essence
Orange icing
2 oz./50 g. luxury margarine*
4 oz./100 g. icing sugar
1 teaspoon orange juice
1–2 oz./25–50 g. chocolate buttons to decorate

AMERICAN
¾ lb. semi-sweet chocolate pieces
½ cup soft margarine*
½ cup granulated sugar
generous 1 cup graham cracker crumbs
1 teaspoon vanilla extract
Orange icing
¼ cup soft margarine*
1 cup sifted confectioners' sugar
1 teaspoon orange juice
⅓ cup chocolate buttons or chips to decorate

*This term is used to describe the soft quick-creaming margarine.

Break the chocolate into pieces, put into a mixing bowl. Place over a saucepan of hot water and allow to melt, then cool. Place the rest of the ingredients in the bowl and beat together with a wooden spoon until well mixed. Place in a 6-inch (15-cm.) round cake tin, previously lined with greaseproof paper and brushed with melted luxury margarine. Smooth the top evenly with the back of a spoon. Place in the refrigerator until set. To make the icing; place all the

ingredients in a mixing bowl and beat until smooth. Carefully lift the cake out of the tin, turn upside down on a plate and remove the greaseproof paper.

Spread a little of the icing on top of the cake and smooth evenly with a palette knife. Place the remaining icing in a piping bag fitted with a star tube and pipe stars around the top edge and in the centre. Place the chocolate buttons at angles between each star and in the centre.

POTATO PAN SCONES

Cooking time: 10 minutes*

Serves 4

IMPERIAL · METRIC	AMERICAN
4 oz./100 g. boiled potatoes	¼ lb. boiled potatoes
4 oz./100 g. self-raising flour	1 cup all-purpose flour sifted with 1 teaspoon baking powder
1 oz./25 g. butter or margarine	2 tablespoons butter or margarine
2 oz./50 g. castor sugar	¼ cup granulated sugar
2–3 oz./50–75 g. dried fruit	½ cup dried fruit
milk to mix	milk to mix
½ oz./15 g. fat	1 tablespoon shortening

*If the potato is ready cooked.

Mash the potatoes or sieve until very smooth. Sieve the flour, rub in butter or margarine, add the sugar and fruit and blend with the potato. Gradually add enough milk to give a firm rolling consistency. Form into a round the size of your strongest frying pan, cut into four triangles. Rub the fat over the pan; warm but do not get too hot. Put in the scones. Cook for approximately 5 minutes on either side over fairly low heat. Test and when firm to the touch they are cooked.

BISCUITS

Biscuits are excellent for tea time, as most biscuits keep well in an airtight tin. A biscuit dough can be kneaded quite vigorously unless stated to the contrary.

Here are the important rules about biscuit making:
1 Do not add too much liquid. Many recipes have no liquid at all. Unless stated to the contrary, bake steadily so they become crisp before they are over-browned.
2 Put on to an ungreased tray unless cheese, oatmeal or syrup has been used in the biscuits.
3 Allow most biscuits to cool on the baking tin. In old recipes they were always baked twice – this is not essential, but if they soften slightly with keeping, crisp them up in a moderate oven for a few minutes.
4 Store away from cakes, pastry or bread.

JANHAGEL

Cooking time: 20–25 minutes
Oven temperature: 375°F., 190°C., Gas Mark 5

Makes 18

IMPERIAL · METRIC	AMERICAN
4 oz./100 g. butter	½ cup butter
6 oz./150 g. plain flour	1½ cups all-purpose flour
2 oz./50 g. castor sugar	¼ cup granulated sugar
½ teaspoon powdered cinnamon	½ teaspoon powdered cinnamon
Topping	**Topping**
1 oz./25 g. flaked blanched almonds (page 69)	¼ cup flaked blanched almonds (page 69)
1 tablespoon granulated sugar	1 tablespoon granulated sugar

Rub the butter into the sieved flour, add the sugar and cinnamon and work together. Press into a buttered Swiss roll tin, flatten with a knife. Sprinkle with the almonds and granulated sugar. Bake in the centre of a moderately hot oven for 20–25 minutes, until golden brown. Cut into fingers while still warm. These biscuits keep well in an airtight tin.

GINGERNUTS

Cooking time: 10–15 minutes
Oven temperature:
350–375°F., 180–190°C.,
Gas Mark 4–5

Makes 12 biscuits

IMPERIAL · METRIC	AMERICAN
4 oz./100 g. plain flour	1 cup all-purpose flour
1 teaspoon powdered ginger	1 teaspoon powdered ginger
½ teaspoon bicarbonate of soda	½ teaspoon baking soda
1 oz./25 g. sugar	2 tablespoons sugar
2 oz./50 g. cooking fat or margarine	¼ cup shortening or margarine
2 tablespoons golden syrup	3 tablespoons maple syrup

Sieve the dry ingredients and add the sugar. Heat the fat and golden syrup until the fat has melted, add to dry ingredients. Divide mixture into 12 pieces and roll into balls. Put on a lightly greased baking sheet, allowing room for the biscuits to spread out. Bake just above the centre of a moderate to moderately hot oven for approximately 10 minutes. At the end of this time the biscuits may not be quite cooked, but turn the heat off so that they cook for a further 5 minutes without danger of burning. Allow to set for 5 minutes on the tin, then lift on to a wire tray.

Janhagel

TOFFEE WALNUT BISCUITS

Cooking time: 10 minutes
Oven temperature:
350–375°F., 180–190°C.,
Gas Mark 4–5

IMPERIAL · METRIC
4 oz./100 g. butter
3 oz./75 g. demerara sugar
1 egg
2 oz./50 g. walnuts, chopped
8 oz./200 g. plain flour
milk (see method)

AMERICAN
½ cup butter
6 tablespoons brown sugar
1 egg
½ cup chopped walnuts
2 cups all-purpose flour
milk (see method)

Makes 18

Cream the butter and sugar until soft, add the egg, nuts and flour. Knead well and if necessary, add a very little milk to bind. Form into a roll about 2 inches (5 cm.) in diameter. Chill in hot weather. Cut about 18 slices with a sharp knife, put on to a greased baking sheet and bake for about 10 minutes in centre of a moderate to moderately hot oven.

Spiced biscuits Use castor instead of brown sugar, sieve ½–1 level teaspoon spice with the flour.
Coconut biscuits Use castor instead of brown sugar and desiccated coconut instead of walnuts.

Supper time

The recipes in various parts of this book will enable you to produce quick snacks for supper. Many of the breakfast dishes can be served with salads or vegetables to make them more interesting and sustaining. Here are a few extra ideas:

Scotch eggs
Follow the directions for cheese Scotch eggs on page 72 but instead of coating the eggs with the cheese mixture coat with sausage meat. You need 12 oz. (300 g.; 1½ cups) sausage meat for a thin coating for 4 hard-boiled eggs. Brush the sausage meat with the beaten egg and then coat in crisp breadcrumbs and fry. You will find the sausage adheres to the eggs better if they are rolled in a small amount of flour first.

COOKING PASTA

Cooking time: 12–20 minutes

Serves 4

IMPERIAL · METRIC	AMERICAN
4–6 oz./100–150 g. pasta	¼–⅓ lb. pasta
2–3 pints/generous 1–1½ litres water	5–7½ cups water
salt to taste	salt to taste
1 oz./25 g. butter or margarine	2 tablespoons butter or margarine

Put the pasta into the boiling water, never add this until the water is boiling, otherwise it can sink to the bottom. Add approximately 1 teaspoon salt. The cooking time will vary – spaghetti takes approximately 12 minutes, but the thick macaroni can take up to 20 minutes. Do not, however, overcook pasta – it should be only just soft. Spaghetti should be held in the hand and lowered into the boiling water. When the ends soften slightly, turn the spaghetti round so the softened parts drop in the water. Continue like this until you can put in all the pasta.

Drain the pasta well, toss in the butter and serve with the sauce, (see pages 53 and 54) and with extra grated Cheddar or Parmesan cheese.

PORK-STUFFED PEPPERS

Cooking time: 45 minutes
Oven temperature:
350–375°F., 180–190°C.,
Gas Mark 4–5

IMPERIAL · METRIC	AMERICAN
4 green peppers	4 green sweet peppers
water	water
1 pint/generous ½ litre white stock or water and 1 chicken stock cube	2½ cups white stock or water and 1 chicken bouillon cube
3 oz./75 g. long-grain rice	scant ½ cup long-grain rice
1 small onion	1 small onion
2 medium-sized tomatoes	2 medium-sized tomatoes
8 oz./200 g. canned pork meat	½ lb. canned pork meat
seasoning	seasoning
1 oz./25 g. crisp breadcrumbs	¼ cup crisp dry bread crumbs
1 oz./25 g. butter	2 tablespoons butter

Cut a slice from each pepper, scoop out the seeds and cores. Put into boiling water and boil for 5 minutes. Put the stock or water and stock cube into another pan. When boiling, add the rice, peeled, grated onion and skinned, chopped tomatoes. Cook without a lid until the rice is soft, which is about 15 minutes; the liquid should have evaporated. Mix with the diced pork and season; pile into the peppers, top with the breadcrumbs and small knobs of butter. Bake for 25 minutes in a buttered pan in the centre of a moderate to moderately hot oven.

Index